Concern for Church Polity and Discipline

Concern for Church Polity and Discipline

Essays on Pastoral Ministry and Communal Authority, 1958–1969

CONCERN: A Pamphlet Series for Questions of Christian Renewal

EDITED BY
Laura Schmidt Roberts

WIPF & STOCK · Eugene, Oregon

CONCERN FOR CHURCH POLITY AND DISCIPLINE
Essays on Pastoral Ministry and Communal Authority, 1958–1969

CONCERN: A Pamphlet Series for Questions of Christian Renewal

Copyright © 2022 Wipf and Stock Publishers. All rights reserved. Except for brief quotations in critical publications or reviews, no part of this book may be reproduced in any manner without prior written permission from the publisher. Write: Permissions, Wipf and Stock Publishers, 199 W. 8th Ave., Suite 3, Eugene, OR 97401.

Wipf & Stock
An Imprint of Wipf and Stock Publishers
199 W. 8th Ave., Suite 3
Eugene, OR 97401

www.wipfandstock.com

PAPERBACK ISBN: 978-1-7252-6101-3
HARDCOVER ISBN: 978-1-7252-6102-0
EBOOK ISBN: 978-1-7252-6103-7

03/16/22

Contents

Series Foreword | vii

Introduction by Laura Schmidt Roberts | xi

Part I: On Pastoral Ministry

1 Second Thoughts on the Pastoral Ministry | 3
   GERALD C. STUDER

2 Marginalia (excerpt, 1958) | 8
   [UNATTRIBUTED]

3 Efficiency in the Church | 11
   A. H. A. BAKKER

4 The Need to Which We Minister | 15
   EDGAR METZLER

5 The Church's One Foundation | 20
   LEWIS BENSON

6 The Preacher and Preaching | 25
   WALTER KLAASSEN

7 Discipleship and Church Order: A Review and Discussion | 36
   WILLIAM KLASSEN

8 New Presbyter Is Old Priest Writ Large | 43
   WALTER KLAASSEN

9 Theological Education for the Believers' Church | 48
   J. Lawrence Burkholder

10 Marginalia (excerpt, 1969) | 69
   Virgil Vogt

Part II: On Communal Authority, "Order," and Discipline

11 *Studies in Church Discipline*: A Review Article | 75
   Elmer Ediger

12 Some Neglected Aspects in the Biblical View of the Church | 86
   William Klassen

13 Postulates Concerning Religious Intentional Ethnic Groups | 101
   Calvin Redekop

14 On Fraternal Admonition | 107
   Balthasar Hubmaier

15 Walking Together in East Africa | 118
   Don Jacobs

16 Dealing with Other People's Sins | 123
   Samuel Shoemaker

Contemporary Responses

17 Toward Ecclesial Practices and Notions of Authority That Embody Radical Hope | 133
   Kimberly Penner

18 The Ecclesial Flesh of Anabaptist Visions | 143
   Isaac S. Villegas

   Appendix: Listing of all *Concern* republication volumes | 153
   Bibliography | 161

Series Foreword to the 2022 Edition

In 1952 a group of seven young American Mennonite intellectuals studying in Europe convened for a two-week theological retreat in Amsterdam to discuss the place of Mennonites in what they saw as the modern, "post-Christendom" world. Most all had come to post-war Europe with Canadian or American Mennonite organizations to assist mission, relief, and rebuilding efforts. They are, in the words of one participant, overwhelmed by what they encounter—the theology, imagery, procedures, and practices they bring are inadequate to their work and witness in postwar Europe. They have many questions about what it means to be the church—to be disciples—in that time and place; questions compounded by conversations and studies that open up for them the ideological and philosophical currents sweeping Europe at the time.

What becomes clear in the papers presented in Amsterdam and the subsequently published series *Concern: A Pamphlet Series for Questions of Christian Renewal* (1954–71) is a common concern over a gap between an Anabaptist vision and contemporary Mennonite reality.[1] They view the increasingly hierarchical denominational structure of the Mennonite church in Canada and the United States and its institution-building as inconsistent with an Anabaptist notion of church as community. These structural forms and the accompanying concerns for their perpetuation reflect "Protestantizing" compromise instead of Anabaptist movement-oriented, mission-minded, evangelical zeal. The writers instead call for a more radical and authentic expression of the Christian life. They call for a renewal that would

---

1. Toews, *Mennonites in American Society*, 232. For more on the historical genesis of *Concern* see the front pieces of Vogt, *Roots of CONCERN*, and Hershberger, "Power, Tradition, and Renewal."

realign the mission, leadership, and organization of the church as well as its relationship to broader society in ways more resonant with the tenets of a culturally-engaged Anabaptism; which is to say, they call for a Mennonite response to modernity which is both faithful to their construal of Anabaptist tradition and appropriate to the times.[2]

While *Concern: A Pamphlet Series for Questions of Christian Renewal* and the movement it inspired address the context of the day, the call issued to discern what it means to be a faithful church in and for the times—ever the church's call—is one we face with growing urgency in today's postmodern context. What theology, imagery, and practices are adequate to the work and witness of disciples in this time and place? What is church *for*? Republishing these essays makes more readily available for this task resources shaped by Anabaptist tradition. The themes and issues the essays raise remain relevant: Christian responsibility in and to the "world," the goal of history, critical engagement with political ideologies and economic theories, global mission and the colonial legacy of Christendom, the unavoidably enculturated nature of lived faith, the gifts of the Spirit, desire for renewed (radicalized?) authentic expressions of faith, Anabaptist-shaped church structure and pastoral leadership, the fraught realities of communal authority and discipline.

But the model the pamphlet series provides is equally important. Especially at its inception, *Concern* was intended to be a forum for works in progress versus polished churchly or academic pieces—a place to test ideas, raise questions, challenge practices, even change one's mind. The pamphlets present articles reflecting varying viewpoints intended to promote discussion, critical reflection, and ultimately transformation of understanding, practices, and structured forms of Christian discipleship. This example of dialog across difference as a shared path toward renewal is welcome in the current increasingly polarized context, where disagreement seems more likely to end a conversation than begin one.

Response essays from contemporary Mennonite writers in each volume continue in this vein, critically engaging the contribution and limitations of the historical essays and building out concerns of their own in the current global, ecclesial, and historical climate. One aspect of that climate is especially important to state clearly: the mixed legacy of *Concern* writer

---

2. See Vogt, "Foreword," in *The Roots of CONCERN*. Sawatsky, "Editorial," iii. *The Conrad Grebel Review* 8.2 contains articles on and reflections by participants in the *Concern* movement.

and sometime editor, theologian and ethicist John Howard Yoder, whose sexual abuse must be acknowledged.³ The depth and breadth of harm Yoder perpetrated, most horrifically on those he abused, and also on the shape and substance of Anabaptist-Mennonite theology and ecclesiology, is difficult to fathom. While significant deconstruction of Yoder's work has been done, grappling with the aftermath and implications continues.⁴ Refusing to engage or promote Yoder's work as a whole or selectively is one avenue of response. Such selectivity is evident in this series; most, but not all, of Yoder's essays have been republished here. Some material already widely available, and especially the content or use of which harmed victim-survivors of Yoder's abuse, has not been included. Another avenue of response takes encounters with his thought (in church, in institutions, in print) as an occasion to reframe discussion of it: by first speaking the truth of his serial sexual abuse and then reconsidering his work in light of that context. This series also does some of that work selectively, at the choice of several contemporary response writers and in this acknowledgment prefacing each volume. *Concern* should not be reduced to Yoder's contributions. While persistent, Yoder's voice is but one among many across the original pamphlets. On their own, the other fifty-plus writers give rich, contextualized, and diverse expression to theological, ecclesiological, and missiological explorations in the mid-twentieth century.

A historical republication project such as this is not possible without the expert help of librarians and archivists. I owe such debts in too many places to name but the greatest—to Fresno Pacific University's Hiebert Library Director Kevin Enns-Rempel, archivist Hannah Keeney, and research librarian David Hasegawa—must be mentioned. I have benefitted from the university's support through a sabbatical leave dedicated to this project, multiple Provost's Faculty Research Grants, and the Fresno Pacific Biblical Seminary's Center for Anabaptist Studies donation toward publication costs. I greatly appreciate other contributions toward those costs from the Schafer-Friesen Research Fund (Goshen College), the Gerhard Lohrenz

---

3. See Waltner Goossen, "'Defanging the Beast.'" Waltner Goossen catalogs both Yoder's serial sexual abuse and institutional failure to respond adequately to his victims or Yoder himself.

4. In addition to the many articles in *Mennonite Quarterly Review* 89.1, see for example Anabaptist Mennonite Biblical Seminary, "AMBS Response to Victims"; Cramer et al., "Theology and Misconduct"; "On Teaching John Howard Yoder" collection of essays by Mennonite faculty from various institutions in *Mennonite Life* 68 (2014); Soto Albrecht and Stephens, eds. *Liberating the Politics of Jesus*.

SERIES FOREWORD TO THE 2022 EDITION

Publication Fund (Canadian Mennonite University), and the Conrad Grebel University College Theological Studies Program. I am especially grateful to the Mennonite Faith and Learning Society (British Columbia), whose work first became known to me through its sponsorship of the Humanitas Anabaptist Centre (Trinity Western University), and whose very generous support of this publication shows concretely their stated commitment to advance education and scholarship from an Anabaptist perspective.

Thanks are due to Fresno Pacific colleagues in the Division of Biblical and Religious Studies, especially Quentin Kinnison, to Rod Janzen, and to Larry Dunn, for unflagging support, probing questions, and insightful feedback along the way. This project would not have come to me without Ched Myers' suggestion and encouragement, and would not have come to completion without the steadfast guidance and input of Ted Lewis at Wipf and Stock. Thank you both for the gift of this work. Finally, I am deeply grateful to the contemporary response writers in each volume of the series whose essays model so well what Paul Ricoeur would call a "refiguring" of tradition. Thank you for grappling with the plurality and ambiguity of tradition in ways that challenge and potentially revitalize it through theology and praxis from and for actual current ecclesial communities, Anabaptist and otherwise.

An appendix in each book in this series lists the contents of the seven total volumes comprising the *Concern* republication project initiated under the editorial direction of Virgil Vogt which this series completes.[5]

Laura Schmidt Roberts
Fresno Pacific University
September 2021

---

5. In addition to this four-volume, thematically organized series, three other volumes complete the Wipf and Stock republication of the *Concern* pamphlets: Vogt, *Roots of CONCERN* and *CONCERN for Education*; Vogt and Roberts, *Concern for Anabaptist Renewal*.

Introduction

This volume draws together *Concern* essays that address shifting models of pastoral ministry and church structures, reconfiguration of pastoral and communal authority, and notions of communal accountability and support as central to discipleship and leadership.[1] Writers explore these issues and developments in light of their construals of sixteenth-century Anabaptism and a broader Believers' Church ecclesiology. Editorial comments accompanying the earliest of these essays when originally published explain that some pastors were scrutinizing the evolving form of "the pastorate"—re-examining "not the fundamental imperative to Christian service and witness, nor the basic reality of vocation to the Christian ministry, but the forms, the accessory attitudes and assumptions which seem often to accompany certain types of ministerial leadership."[2] They rejected the "determinism" of the church-sect typology by which gradual cultural accommodation means the sect becomes "the typical captive denomination" (the church). They wanted the training and education but not the hierarchical, clergy-laity split. Polity and discipline emerge as two primary points of conversation as they work to develop a "third-way" vision of ministry and ecclesiology for their day. They do so engaging broader ecumenical conversations around these issues.

The first section, "On Pastoral Ministry," begins with essays from 1958–61 that challenge the emergence of centralized, professionalized, pastoral ministry and the resultant changes in polity and practices. The articles critically assess the shift from a multiple-person ministry to a (Protestant)

---

1. For the origins and context of *Concern: A Pamphlet Series for Questions of Christian Renewal* (1954–71) please see the Series Foreword to this volume.
2. "Marginalia," 46–49.

mono-pastorate role, concluding that the "professionalization" of pastoral ministry and the resultant clergy-laity split are fundamentally incompatible with a Believers' Church ecclesiology. They argue, in contrast, that a reclamation of the priesthood of all believers is the path of Christian renewal. While essays from the original *Concern* 17 (1969) were written later, they reflect similar lines of criticism and develop an even more robust vision of the "nonprofessional" priesthood of the community of faith.

The second grouping of essays, "On Communal Authority, 'Order' and Discipline," focuses on one particular aspect of this discussion, the community's authority and obligation to pursue a disciplined life together as characteristic of a Believers' Church ecclesiology. As writers contrast sixteenth-century Anabaptist ecclesiology to that of the Reformers, church discipline repeatedly comes to the fore as a central feature. Elmer Ediger reviews the Mennonite Church authorized volume *Studies in Church Discipline* (1958) which calls for a return to "the brotherhood church" in contrast to "watered-down Protestantism." William Klassen (1960) distinguishes features of sixteenth-century Anabaptist ecclesiology from those of the Reformers, clarifying the biblical bases for the Believers' Church understandings of the identity and mission of the church, and providing lengthy discussion of church discipline as a central. Sociologist Calvin Redekop (1961) puts forward several postulates regarding the interrelationship of church discipline, intentional religious community, and ethnic identity, concluding an inverse relation between these factors and capacity for outreach and perpetuation of beliefs. Articles from the original *Concern* 14 (1967) reassert the community's authority to "bind and loose," reclaiming a robust practice of the disciplined priesthood of all believers in contrast to the sharp clergy-laity split characteristic of professionalized mono-pastorate models as critiqued in the first section of this volume.

Two response essays conclude the volume. Kimberly Penner affirms the importance of the questions the historical essays wrestle with—how Anabaptist-Mennonites understand the relationship between pastoral and congregational authority, what kind of discipline the church is called to practice. Today, she observes: "Existing and historical notions of ecclesial authority and church discipline for Anabaptist-Mennonites have been re-evaluated with a critical eye for relationships of unequal power within the congregation in light of the experiences of Mennonites who have been marginalized, excluded, oppressed, and/or experienced violence within the church itself." As a result, Penner calls for notions of pastoral and communal authority that name and subvert relationships of unequal, top-down power, asserting that the interpersonal and social systemic nature of privilege must be understood as it pertains to relationships *within* the community of faith. In his response, Isaac Villegas notes that the historical essays focus not on church "programs" but on discerning institutional forms that "attend to the routines and rituals of a communal movement," the material practices structuring a shared life. His essay critiques abstracted, idealized, essentialized renderings of Anabaptism, instead approaching actual ecclesial bodies as "indispensable articulations of Anabaptist identities." His exploration of an Anabaptist "ecclesial flesh" for today presents a priesthood of all believers which makes concrete biblical nonviolence, radical hospitality, and persistent attention to power dynamics within communities of faith.

Finally, readers should know that two writings originally part of *Concern*'s robust discussion of these matters have not been republished here. John Howard Yoder's "Binding and Loosing," a self-described "study outline" of Matt 18:15–20 and interpretation of its meaning for discipline, reconciliation, and forgiveness in the church, informed the flawed accountability processes in response to Yoder's sexual abuse which further harmed victims. Yoder himself used this work to manipulate those processes, including demanding an audience with those who experienced and reported his abuse. The articles from the original *Concern* 14 (1967, Hubmaier, Jacobs, Shoemaker) which close the second section of this volume are the historical context in which that full writing first appeared in print. Yoder republished the piece as part of the book *Body Politics* in 1992, the same year charges of sexual misconduct against him made the newspapers and initiated a disciplinary process.[3] Our context is one in which re-presenting this writing risks retraumatizing victim-survivors of Yoder and of other sexual abusers, many of whom still await justice.

Yoder's "The Fullness of Christ," appeared in *Concern* 17 (1969), developed from an earlier presentation to the InterSeminary Movement at the Ecumenical Institute in Evanston, Illinois. The text engages ecumenical discussions of pastoral ministry and church polity of its time, critiquing

---

3. *The Elkhart* (Indiana) *Truth* religion writer, Tom Price, published a five-part series of investigative articles July 12–16, 1992. For discussion of this second formal disciplinary process Yoder underwent, see Waltner Goossen, "'Defanging the Beast,'" 60–73. For detailed critical examination of Yoder's work on "binding and loosing" and its supporting problematic ecclesiology see Villegas, "Ecclesial Ethics," 191–214. Yoder's original article remains available through reference libraries that carry the *Concern* historical pamphlets.

the mono-pastorate "religious specialist" model and arguing instead for a "universality of ministry" as the New Testament apostolic vision. In this view all in the congregation have gifts to exercise for the benefit of the community; "the pastorate" is but one among this universality of ministry marking the diverse body of Christ. The lengthy essay's broadest influence began two decades later. It was an invited plenary presentation for the Believers' Church Conference on Ministry (1987), was published as a book under the same title with minor revisions at that time, and remains widely available.[4] As with all of Yoder's work, its contribution to ongoing Anabaptist-Mennonite theology and practice must be reconsidered in the full context of what we now know is a troublingly mixed legacy.

---

4. Yoder, *Fullness of Christ*. Yoder's original article remains available through reference libraries that carry the *Concern* historical pamphlets.

Part I

On Pastoral Ministry

1

Second Thoughts on the Pastoral Ministry

Gerald C. Studer

For some time, I have had a growing concern and not a few doubts about the type of ministry the Mennonite Church is falling heir to. We seem to study many things most carefully in an effort to be thoroughly biblical and true to our historic traditions, but I see little evidence that this is true in the case of our view of the ministry. We are more concerned about placement and tenure than we are about whether we have a biblical doctrine of the church after placement has been made and tenure established. Are we straining at gnats and swallowing a camel?

I am a first-class example of the thing that concerns me. I am a full-time salaried minister. I sometimes think congregational and denominational chore-boy would describe my work better. I don't mean to be facetious in suggesting this. Nor am I blaming the congregation in saying this. I believe the fault lies in the nature of the polity we are following. It is no time for irony and sarcasm. Paul was willing to be all things to all men, but did he mean by this that he was to do all things for all men?

Can members of a brotherhood make decisions that are God's will for our generation unless they are personally involved in the decision-making process? Will approval of the work of a committee suffice? Do we imply that most church members are such babes in Christ that they cannot be trusted to arrive at a Scriptural solution without seminary training and official installation in a position of responsibility? What is our doctrine of the Holy Spirit? I find no fault with the existence of duly ordained and salaried ministers, but I do have doubts about the growing number of duties and decisions and responsibilities that are either assigned to them or are taken by them. I have no objections to an association of churches in a conference, but in the working of the conference machinery and the time required of some men away from their congregations inclines me to believe that Franklin Clark Fry stated it about right when he said: "The Lord called me into the ministry and the church called me away from it." When it is reported that a layman answered a brother's request of him to help at a task in the congregation with the words, "Get the preacher to do that. That's what we are paying him for!"—my heart sinks within me and I ask myself, "Is that really what the pastor is being paid for?" This may be what that particular brother understands of the minister's task, but is that the New Testament's understanding of the minister's task? How many other people in our congregations think this way?

The King James Version translates Eph 4:11–12 like this: "And he gave some, apostles; and some, prophets; and some, evangelists; and some, pastors and teachers; for the perfecting of the saints, for the work of the ministry, for the edifying of the body of Christ." Most people have taken the last verse to give a threefold outline of the pastor's work. The passage really intends to tell us nothing of the sort. In the first place, it says, pastors and teachers. Furthermore, I believe we must consult other versions to get the more accurate translation of this passage's real meaning. Paul is saying, by the inspiration of the Holy Spirit, that God gave some to be ministers and teachers "with a view to the equipment of the saints for their (i.e. the saints') work of ministering."

Our society is of such a nature today that we need a sprinkling of men throughout the church who are academically trained in certain areas of church work and biblical study just as we need especially trained mechanics and doctors and lawyers to help us at times when it would be practically impossible for us to help ourselves. We cannot all know and experience everything. There are men gifted in this way, and others in that way and I see no New Testament objection in paying them in order that they may have time free in the exercise of their gifts. But this requires a more precise division of responsibility than we have arrived at to date.

What I do object to is the growing gulf between minister and people both in the understanding of many problems and in the outworking of them. We are in danger of asking our congregations to rubber stamp our personal decision or a committee's decision without giving them the painful privilege of growing with us through the decision-making process.

Furthermore, must we conclude that because the multiple lay ministry has brought us many grievous problems in the past, that it is now time to turn to a single and trained ministry, exclusively? (By lay ministry here I mean an untrained ministry, not an unordained ministry.) Any system of ministry, whether singular or plural, will operate no more smoothly than the spirituality of the congregations involved will allow. We may take a shortcut in arriving at an immediate outcome, but we will never find a shortcut to the coming to "the unity of the faith, and of the knowledge of the Son of God, unto a perfect (mature) man, unto the measure of the stature of the fulness of Christ; that we henceforth be no more children" (Eph 4:13–14).

Until recently most, if not all, of our conferences consisted of the ordained brethren only. More recently, a few of the conferences have widened their official membership to include a lay delegate from each congregation. I suppose the members of every constituent congregation have always considered themselves conference members, but they were so only via their ordained leadership. I simply bring this up in order to call to our attention the truth of a statement made by G. A. Jacob in his book entitled *The Ecclesiastical Polity of the New Testament*:

> But the word (church) is never used in the New Testament to . . . mean Christian ministers as distinguished from the general body of Christians. On the contrary, in two instances, it is found to signify the laity or general body as distinguished from the apostles and elders; thus "they were received of the church, and of the apostles and elders," and it pleased "the apostles and elders, with the whole church," who are afterwards in the same chapter designated as "the apostles and elders and brethren."[1]

I have no objection to conferences (indeed, I see much need for them), but I do wonder whether we have not tended too much to forget that such advisory and counseling bodies exist in subordination to and for the purpose of the orderly spread of the gospel and the administration of the local congregations. I am inclined to suspect that the growing tendency to think of the conferences as the church is a warning to us that we are moving in a hierarchical direction that is totally contrary to our Anabaptist and Scriptural heritage.

Another indication of this may be a tendency in some conferences and congregations to replace deacons with stewards, and an eldership with a church council. I do not mean to dicker about words and titles, but I

---

1. Jacob, *Ecclesiastical Polity*, 10.

have to doubt whether this is all the replacement means. The early church ordained elders in every church and deacons were ordained too. I doubt whether any person, no matter how talented or consecrated, can properly fulfill his calling if he is installed into a very circumscribed office and for only a very short term of office.

Mr. Jacob further writes that "the laity in general were in apostolic and following times much consulted and had great influence in church matters, until priestly pretensions and pride had pushed them aside. Lay, or ruling-elders, may . . . still be very useful for preventing or restraining the growth of hierarchical propensities."[2]

Surely the singular ministry is especially liable to take us in a hierarchical direction unless something be done to prevent it. What is needed in order to meet the crying wants of the present age is not so much an increase in church officials or an increase in the responsibilities and authority of a few as is the sound and self-denying unofficial ministrations of Christian men and women.

The danger was apparently felt already in apostolic times, for Peter writes that presbyters are not to assume too high an authority by lording it over their people. In some of the Epistles, indeed, churches are addressed and admonished without any notice at all being taken of their ministers, who remain undistinguished in the general body, as in Romans and Galatians. In some, the presence of ministers is acknowledged, but with only a passing allusion, if any, to the nature of their office, as in Ephesians and Philippians. In one, a message is sent to a minister, through the church, bidding him take heed to his ministry, that he fulfills it, as in Colossians. Yet I would not be misunderstood, for it is also clear that churches are expressly bidden to revere and obey their ministers and in the pastoral epistles Timothy and Titus are strongly urged to assert their authority. A careful consideration of what is due from the clergy to the laity, and from the laity to the clergy (if we may use the terms), would not be unprofitable at the present time.

It is perhaps also not out of order to call our attention to another fact indicated by the New Testament which we overlook as we take current practice quite for granted. The New Testament nowhere presents the Christian ministry as necessary on account of certain spiritual functions which could not otherwise have been lawfully discharged. There are positively no sacred rites or acts which it is declared in the New Testament must be administered by men ordained, or in any way separated from the general

---

2. Jacob, *Ecclesiastical Polity*, 57.

body of believers. Yet the New Testament does call for the doing of things "decently and in order" (1 Cor 14:40). There was no spiritual act which in itself was of such a nature that it might not have been done by every individual Christian, but the general well-being and healthy action of the whole body suggests that known and responsible persons should be charged with certain religious duties in the midst of it. Presence aptly remarks that the words of Paul to the Corinthians imply that all Christians might break the bread and bless the cup at the Lord's Supper, and not an officiating minister only; for, he says, "the bread which we break," and "the cup which we bless" (1 Cor 10:16). It is certainly doubtful that Paul was using the editorial or pastoral plural. Our own church in Switzerland began by the mutual baptizing of each other by those few gathered together in prayer and Bible study. While some organization and agreed-upon assignment of responsibilities is necessary to the orderly life of the church, perhaps we have allowed hierarchical propensities to increase the number of these unduly.

As if to show beyond dispute that official ministerial functions and unofficial popular influence were quite compatible, and ought to be in active, harmonious, and general exercise in the church, the two are united in a remarkable manner in a single utterance by Paul when he writes thus to the Thessalonians: "Wherefore comfort yourselves together (better, exhort yourselves together), and edify one another, even as also ye do. And we beseech you, brethren, to know them which labor among you, and are over you in the Lord, and admonish you; and to esteem them very highly in love for their work's sake. And be at peace among yourselves. Now we exhort you, brethren, warn (same word as translated admonish a few lines before when spoken of the ministers) them that are unruly, comfort" (1 Thess 5:11–14).

I have written these lines in the conviction that we honestly want to recover the Anabaptist and biblical vision and not merely talk and write about it. I believe it is time we stop and take stock of our way before we continue blindly down a path that leads us farther and farther from our desired goal. If these warnings prove to be unnecessary, no one will be happier than I for this reassurance. If they are found to be more true than anticipated, then let us realign ourselves more precisely with our desired goal. No polity will ensure spirituality, but some polities are surely more conducive to true spirituality than others.

2

Marginalia (excerpt, 1958)

[UNATTRIBUTED]

The article by Gerald Studer is the first of several which have been promised to *Concern* on the conception of the "pastorate" as it has evolved in recent years. This scrutiny is being turned on the pastorate by men who stand within it, having been trained for it. They have come to re-examine not the fundamental imperative to Christian service and witness, nor the basic reality of vocation to the Christian ministry, but the forms, the accessory attitudes and assumptions which seem often to accompany certain types of ministerial leadership.

The various efforts of sociologists attempting to reduce the history of Christian groups to typical patterns seem to place any church before a pair of alternatives. There is the "sect-type" ministry, composed of men called by the church or arising spontaneously from the midst of her membership. Such ministers may be gifted with considerable insight and leadership capacity and some self-acquired education, but they are typically without extensive formal training and their financial support is generally not secured with any contractual certainty. In the other, "church-type" pattern, ministerial training and support are guaranteed institutionally, whether by the State, as in much of Europe's history, or by voluntary associations. The "ministry" is one of the "professions," comparable in training and prestige if not in remuneration with medicine, teaching, and the law. A young person decides to study for the ministry as he would for any other livelihood. The ministry as thus conceived is not above all the prophetic leadership of a pilgrim people, but one of the stable institutional elements of a healthy society.

[UNATTRIBUTED]—MARGINALIA (EXCERPT, 1958)

The lesson of history seems to be clearly that the transition from the spontaneously chosen and supported to the regularly trained and salaried ministry marks an important step in the "sect-cycle," i.e., in that gradual process of accommodation to and acceptance by secular society by way of which the typical Free Church becomes the typical captive denomination.

To accept from deterministic sociology this framework of types and cyclical development patterns would be to become "captive to the elements of this world." But to refuse to admit any significance to patterns which have undeniably been observed and to think that one is automatically and without effort delivered from them by virtue of faith would be to refuse to perceive the warnings of history and thereby to condemn oneself to follow that same pattern. There is no logical or theological incompatibility between trained and supported ministers and the disciples' church. Both doctrinal training and financial support under certain conditions are called for by the New Testament, in a context where Christians were by no means what sociologists would type as a mass church. Yet after nineteen centuries the burden of proof lies with those who hope that organized means of training and support can make in the life of today's churches an impact diametrically opposite to the trends with which they have been correlated in the past.

This is a burden of proof which we must assume. The training and the support of servants of the church are imperatives both biblically and in view of our day's needs and challenges. We must therefore refuse to accept the alternatives with which sociologists present us. Yet when we enter this realm it should be with fear and trembling, in the full awareness that what we are attempting has always failed before. There operate in this realm certain drives toward autonomy, certain potentialities for demonic rebellion of the instrument against its purpose, which have generally tended to put the "clergy" as a class on the wrong side when the renewal of the church was at stake. The training of servants of the church is a realm which must be exorcised. Not only do certain terms ("clergy," "laity," "reverend," "full-time Christian service") need serious re-examination and possible repudiation; even more do the unspoken and even unconscious presuppositions of teachers, students, and congregations need to be purged of attitudes borrowed from the mass churches.

Such an exorcism and creative reappraisal would be much more demanding than the task, sufficiently great in itself, of creating and winning acceptance for seminaries of the general Protestant type; yet without the higher and harder goal the other is of questionable value. Such creativity as is being called for here is all the more imperative in view of the fact that Christendom in general, especially outside of America, both in Europe (the birthplace of the parish pattern) and in the "young churches," is seeking to restore some of the values maintained by the ministerial patterns of the free-church tradition. Catholic priests are supporting themselves in order to restore their parishioners' respect for the validity of the ministry. Protestant pastors are laboring to recreate a sense of lay responsibility for leadership including preaching; in East Germany because the pastoral system is especially vulnerable to persecution, in West Germany and Switzerland because they have lost their contact with and the respect of the masses whom their inherited definition of the church says they are there to serve. This would seem to be the least appropriate time of all for encouraging or riding along un-critically with the change of landslide proportions which is taking place in Mennonite conceptions of the ministry. Further discussions of this issue will be welcomed.

3

Efficiency in the Church

A. H. A. Bakker

The financial experts of our brotherhood have recently computed how much a minister costs per year. It is their intention that every congregation shall face these facts. We should see these things as they are. We should know that a minister is too great a burden for one small congregation alone, so that we must combine more and more small congregations. The larger congregations can pay their ministers adequately only if they give them responsibilities too large to be discharged properly. It is good that we know these things. But this should bring us to examine whether this expensive minister is being used in the most efficient way.

What is the task of the minister in the congregation? In short, it is expected of him that he be the center around which the congregation revolves; he should feed the members spiritually, sharing their joys and their needs, and by this contact with them he should be the binding power in the congregation. To be able to do this, he should be a spiritually alert person who knows deep personal fellowship with God and who can meet his fellow men with understanding and love. He should have knowledge about theological questions and should have insight into human character and an awareness of what is happening in the world. During his studies he began to acquire the insight necessary for these needs. But if he wants to grow into what a preacher should be—a teacher of religion and a spiritual adviser—then he should have time for prayer and studying, and he should have regular contact with people with whom he feels himself united in these concerns.

What will come of all this in a normal minister's life? There is so much to do to keep the congregation together and moving that the minister does not get the chance to become what he should be. In most cases he cannot do what he knows is expected of him. All this is the cause of much inner tension and dissatisfaction and frustration which will further reduce his effectiveness. The present state of congregational life demonstrates that this way of working is unfavorable for the minister and for the congregation.

Where lies the fault? If a business firm has in its service an experienced technician, the firm will be wise enough to let this man do his own work because only thus is he worth his salary. They do not pay him to do work for which he is not trained and which he cannot do expertly. This is, however, what our congregations are doing with their ministers. Both congregation and minister feel that this arrangement is not working well, and therefore it is being said that ministerial training is unsatisfactory and should be on a broader basis. But it is impossible to teach a man in a limited period enough about theology that he may call himself a theologian and besides all this still teach him enough about psychology, pedagogy, sociology, administration, and financial management which he will need for a minister's work. To attempt to do this would unavoidably produce that dangerous kind of people who know just barely enough about anything and nothing really well. And our churches will not be well served with this!

I would like to plead for another solution to this problem. I see it as urgently necessary that as congregations and ministers we rid ourselves of the idea that the congregation is a kind of one-man business directed by the minister. The congregation is the business of the whole congregation. There is much work to be done to keep it together which can be done just as well by any active member as by the minister. I am thinking of normal visitation which helps to keep the members united, the education of the youth, church social evenings, deaconate work, administrative work, finances, and the care of the church buildings. In all these fields the minister has the same skills as his members; in many of them the minister knows less than some of his members, who by their training and daily work are experts in a certain field. And if it might happen that he has learned more about it, then this has happened at the expense of his expertness in his own field.

It certainly shows a wrong attitude among us Mennonites if a visit made in the name of the church only counts if it is made by the pastor. It would be better for the unity of the church if the members themselves could do this work. A talk given by one of the members to an evening meeting on a subject in which he is interested can lead to thinking and talking together just as well or even better than a lecture given by the minister. It seems to me that it might be a good thing for churches which share one minister if the Sunday morning service were conducted by a brother or sister from the congregation while the minister preached in the other church, rather than meeting only when the pastor can be present. But could our members do this? I am convinced that in our churches enough people can be found capable of taking over a great part of the work now done by the minister, if they only thought themselves capable.

But for some aspects of this work a spiritual insight is needed—a conscious religious life which many of our members lack. They know this and are afraid of a task for which they do not feel spiritually qualified. Right here lies the work for which the minister has been training: to give insight in questions of faith and to help with thinking through the consequences of faith in all the different areas of life. As it is now, this is not asked of him often enough. There are not many people who are willing to give of their time for deep-going spiritual training. They do not see of what use it could be.

But if it should come so far that the congregation would call upon her members to work actively, then such training would be seen to be a necessity, instead of a kind of superfluous luxury. This would be important for the workers and for the minister—for the former group because it would strengthen their spiritual life and for the latter because it would find people with whom he could explore the different facets of faith.

The ADS (Dutch Mennonite Conference) is earnestly studying how it might be possible to train people in our brotherhood to be co-workers in the congregation. They are thinking of a kind of lay training center. But should not every parsonage be such a center? The local pastor remains as teacher of those with whom he works; they know the mutual field of work which is the congregation, and they can judge together the results of the work. Only in the local congregation can a circle of people grow who actually do the work in mutual responsibility. We should not train solitary workers; we must rather form a group of people who grow together toward more positive faith and more efficient service.

This will set high standards for the minister who should be a real spiritual leader and who will have to remain this for the persons with whom he works so closely. He will have to forsake some activities in which he now can lose himself, activities in which he can be very much the "parson," but in which he is not spiritually what he should be. But he will also be enabled to concentrate on the task for which he has been prepared; he no longer needs to be a handy man. Nor is it any longer necessary that he be the man with whom the congregation stands or falls (which, of course, in reality he never is, but he can imagine that he is, and the congregation usually is quite ready to strengthen him in this fancy). He now carries a shared responsibility; he is a co-worker. He is now in a situation which offers better chances for the development of his own personality, not to speak of his spiritual welfare, than in the present situation with its dangers of loneliness and vanity.

But not only for the minister has this system its advantages. It will be for the benefit of the congregation if in her midst there is formed a nucleus of persons who, out of a positively experienced faith, carry together the life of the congregation and who work each according to his own ability. Church membership itself will win a new value and dignity if it can lead to this responsibility.

These thoughts are offered in the hope that a way may be found out of the *impasse* in which we find ourselves concerning the ministry in our brotherhood. I know that we are not alone in facing this problem. But we will have to try to find a solution which fits our own situation. This situation has grown out of our own history. We started out with a ministry which arose out of the local church itself and worked under the leadership of elders responsible for several congregations. Following the pattern of other denominations, we then formed a "corps" of university men and women because our forefathers saw the utility of trained spiritual leaders. But we have thereby degenerated—as it has been said before—into a "preachers' church." We now are top-heavy with leadership (speaking financially). But our ministers are overloaded, and our congregations no longer know that being a church means being a community of faith and work.

This can and must change if we try in brotherly love and careful consideration to find a way out and if we are willing to break with wrong traditions and go this new way.

4

The Need to Which We Minister

EDGAR METZLER

One needs no special powers of observation to know that the concept and function of the minister in the Mennonite Church are undergoing extensive change. Witness our confusion on problems of placement and tenure, the growing use of titles that have connotations foreign to our theology of the church, and the highly competitive search for pastoral talent by ministerial committees of local congregations.

The exact nature and extent of this change are not clear. One of the more disturbing aspects of the situation is the small amount of study and discussion, especially on the local congregational level, of the implications of the new concepts of ordained leadership. The changing attitudes toward the ministry do not seem to be the result of careful study and prayerful planning on the part of anyone.

In this respect our church shares the general confusion in Protestantism regarding the ministry. In contrast to ecclesiastical tradition, the changing role for the minister is now determined primarily by reflection on the contemporary experience of the church and the needs of men in a complex modern society. The impact of immense cultural and sociological changes inevitably gives rise to new problems and old ones in new forms. (Man's ultimate problems do not change, but in each generation, they present themselves in different form.) Urbanization, industrialization, the fragmentation of life, the ever-increasing organizational complexity, and our deep involvement in it—all these help to shape the form of the church's ministry. Within this matrix of change and challenge, the demands upon the ministry are bound to change also.

The old patterns no longer seem adequate to meet this new situation. As church organization (in the manner of most organizations) abounds in prolific activities and programs, the total endeavor soon becomes too much for informal, part-time administration. The answer has been to secure a pastor, adequately trained and supported, who will give full time to the work of the church. It is expected that he will be competent in preaching, worship leadership, Christian education, personal counseling, and administration. He is usually considered both the spiritual and administrative leader of the congregation. H. Richard Niebuhr has given the name of "pastoral director" to this emerging conception of the ministry.[1]

In addition to the general cultural and religious forces within our North American society which push us toward a new concept of the ministry, there are other factors which may operate to a greater degree than we realize. Much of the pressure for a different kind of ministry may be simply the desire to be like "the church across the street." As the process of absorbing cultural traits reaches increasingly into every area of life, it is to be expected that our norms for church life shall be taken from the experience of Protestantism in general.

It is only natural that our concept of pastors should follow the lines taken by Baptist, Methodist, Presbyterian, and other non-Catholic churches. The texts used in our schools for courses in pastoral theology are written from the perspective of these traditions. My point here is not to argue the validity of these concepts of the pastor, but I want to point out that uncritical acceptance of the commonly assumed role of the pastor in other denominations is one of the factors giving rise to the demand for such a pastor in our local congregations.

But the point of this paper is to suggest that the main reason for the demand for the type of pastor suggested above lies much deeper. The role of the pastor as it is developing in many Mennonite congregations is determined (unconsciously) by those personal needs which are the result of a breakdown of community in general and of brotherhood in particular.

The breakdown of a sense of community in our society is a theme that has preoccupied the social scientists for the past decade. The diagnosis of a sick society resulting from social disintegration has been made again and again simply because the symptoms are so obvious. This cultural disintegration in turn breeds a sense of individual isolation. Modern moral philosophy, theology, the novel, and the theater reflect the frantic efforts

---

1. Niebuhr, *Purpose*, chapter 2.

of modern man to find some sense of relatedness. The gap between the individual and those social relationships in which goals and purposes take on meaning grow wider and wider. The whole context of interpersonal relationships has become distorted and blighted.

The effect of all this on man's spiritual capabilities is, of course, shattering. There is probably less exaggeration than we like to admit in this statement from Robert Nisbet's book *The Quest for Community* (which is mainly an essay of political theory on the development of the modern state),

> the decline of community in the modern world has as its inevitable religious consequences the creation of masses of helpless, bewildered individuals who are unable to find solace in Christianity, regarded merely as creed. The stress upon the individual, at the expense of the churchly community, has led to the isolation of the individual, to the shattering of the man-God relationship, and to the atomization of personality.[2]

An interesting, but tragic, corroboration of this is found in the well-known research of the French sociologist, Durkheim, regarding the comparative rates of suicide in our modern civilization. He found that suicide rates vary inversely with the degree of integration in society. How ironic that among those categories listed as having the highest rate of suicide (urban dwellers, industrial workers, and the unmarried) should also be included those who are members of the Protestant churches.

The deteriorating effects of the decline of community have certainly been reflected in the changing viewpoints and orientation of the social scientists, particularly the psychologists. The old rationalist view of autonomous, self-sufficient man is giving way. Replacing it is a view of man as unstable and inadequate when cut off from social membership or clear belief. Personality itself is being interpreted as an aspect of interpersonal relationships.[3]

We could go on and on observing the loss of community in our society. But what concerns us immediately is the effect of this on the church. The members of the body of Christ are in the world even though they are not of the world. Their citizenship is in another kingdom, but they are buffeted by the storms of this kingdom through which they travel as pilgrims and strangers. If there is any validity at all in the analysis offered

---

2. Nisbet, *Quest*, 259.

3. See particularly the works of Harry Stack Sullivan—for example, *The Interpersonal Theory*.

above, it will readily be seen that the floods that have washed away the main aspects of community in our society in general will also erode the sense of brotherhood in the church.

The broken community at large inevitably places strain and stress on the brotherhood that centers in the church. The members of our congregations are caught up in the individualistic, self-seeking ambitions of their neighbors and coworkers. He becomes involuntarily involved in schemes for security foisted upon him by the welfare state and is constantly invited to participate in others provided by private insurance. No man can participate in such a society without serious consequences to his values and convictions. He finds it difficult to relate in any meaningful way to the body of believers partly because it is not really necessary for him to do so and still live. The brotherhood is less important to him. Certainly, there are many reasons for the breakdown of true brotherhood in our church, but foremost among them must be the fact of our situation in a society which has lost its sense of community.

A member of the church who finds himself in the situation described above may soon also discover the tragedy of it. Or perhaps he may never consciously discover it, but the deleterious effects of the process go on, nonetheless. He no longer needs the brotherhood for his purely physical needs. But man cannot live by bread alone. Cut off from the vitality of the sort of interpersonal relationships found only in the body of Christ that is expressing its full brotherhood, a man's spirit perishes as surely as would his body without oxygen. Many church members are not conscious or do not recognize the symptoms of this soul-sickness which results from a breakdown of brotherhood. But instinctively they reach for help.

Here is where the pastor enters the picture again. He is expected to substitute, at least in part, for the lack of relatedness to the members of the congregation. He becomes the one to whom the members go with their problems. With no opportunity to confess their faults one to another, they go to the pastor-counselor to get rid of their guilt. Without the advantage of admonition and counsel from their brother, the pastor becomes the source of advice.

This is not meant to depreciate pastoral counseling. My own experience convinces me of the necessity and potential effectiveness of it. Furthermore, since most counseling has to do in one way or another with broken relationships, the pastor can do much to restore real community through counseling. When the pastor helps one person, he helps many. Carroll Wise has said that one of the functions of counseling should be to remove barriers to fellowship and that this will help create a sense of Christian community.[4]

But counseling can only be a stopgap measure. If the source of our difficulties is the broken community, then something must be done about the inadequate interpersonal relationships which have corroded the brotherhood. No amount of pastoral leadership will substitute. The ill effects of a weak and diluted brotherhood are only met adequately by a restored and vital brotherhood.

There are certain situations in which the pastor can represent to the individual the fellowship of the church. The symbolic function of the pastor can definitely have a therapeutic effect upon people in need. However, it must be remembered that this function of the pastor is symbolic, and that it must point to a reality behind the symbol. If the reality of a loving, concerned fellowship of Christian believers is not present, the pastor is only the symbol of an illusion. How often pastors have heard this response from a counselee, "Yes, I know what you say is true, but I've never experienced it in this church." Regardless of how well-trained, or how attractive and competent the pastor may be, he can never substitute for the actuality of a vital brotherhood which embraces each member, and by the quality of its life, is a compelling invitation for others to accept its Lord.

The background of Alan Paton's novel *Cry the Beloved Country* is the shattering of the solidarity of a South African community by the forces of industrialization. The story is of the confusion of an African minister whose only son is executed for having committed most of the crimes against society. The community exacts its terrible toll on the family. In one place the consternation of the people in South Africa is expressed in these words, "The counselors of the broken tribe having counsel for everything except the matter of a broken tribe." Wayne Oates comments on this: "Religious counselors tend to have counsel for everything except the matter of the shattered state of the relationships of religious people to each other."

The task of healing the broken community is not easy. A revival of reality in brotherhood is even more difficult. But is this not our central problem in the renewal of the church in our generation? The test of any emerging concept of the pastorate is how much it contributes to the solution of that problem.

---

4. Wise, *Pastoral Counseling*.

5

The Church's One Foundation

Lewis Benson

Christ is the church's one foundation. Christ is the cornerstone. In apocalyptic language, he is the stone cut out of the mountain without hands. This means the church is not a man-made institution. "The church of Christ's communion," says George Fox, "is not in that which proceeds from men below, but in that which proceeds from God and His Son."

But, says Fox,

> a few ages after the apostles . . . Christendom ran . . . from Christ, the way to God after the ways that men had made and from the religion that is pure from above after the religion that men have made. . . . Christ saith, if the truth hath made you free, then are you free indeed, and all religions, ways, and worships are in bondage, . . . it is Christ the truth that doth set free. . . . All that are freemen are made free by the truth, they are God's freemen, they are free citizens, they are free . . . in an everlasting kingdom . . . free in the heavenly city Jerusalem which is from above.[1]

In this community that is not from men below but from God and his Son are God's free citizens of a heavenly city. This is the noninstitutional church of the apocalyptic vision. But, says the practical churchman, unless the church is on her guard, she will be at the mercy of those who take advantage of this freedom, and tempt her to seek liberty on some other foundation.

---

1. Fox, *Works*, 7:311.

There is much at stake. If our freedom in Christ is gone, then we are in bondage again. Fox warns, "Stand up for your liberty in the Gospel and in the faith which Christ hath been the author of for if you lose it, or let another spirit get over you, ye will not soon regain it."[2]

When this danger appears, our human, religion-making instincts lead us to set up bulwarks to protect the liberty and the faith of which Christ is the author. Men look for some objective authority to enforce dependence on Christ. These objective standards are not peculiar to Christianity. They belong to religion in general. They consist of authoritative sacred writings, traditions, rituals, and hierarchical leadership based on historical succession. Behind these bulwarks the practical churchman feels secure.

It cannot be denied that creedal orthodoxy can be maintained by these devices, and freedom which is not in Christ can be excluded. However, this is only part of the story. For as the church strives to keep Christ at the center by devices borrowed from general religion and the old covenant, she finds that this very policy alters the whole character of the Christian community. The unique charismatic quality disappears and with it the unique freedom of the Christian man.[3]

Instead of being the holy city come down from above the church becomes a man-made religious institution. Now the question arises: Does the church have authority to deal with those who would draw her away to some other foundation? Authority belongs to Christ, but how does Christ exercise his authority in his church?

Fox answers that Christ's authority is not mediated through Bible, creed, or priestly hierarchy, but through the continuous encounter of the church with its living ruler and governor. When the church fails to obey Christ's voice or lends its ear to other voices, then the presence and power of Christ fades and the church loses the authority it derives from Christ. The church's safeguard, provided in the new covenant to prevent such falling away, is charismatic leadership. This is not something extraneous to the gospel order. It is the built-in safety device of the new covenant.

What steps can the church take to insure a steady supply of charismatic leaders? No institutional machinery can be depended upon. But the church can do something. First, it can keep close to the prophetic tradition by the study of the Bible. Charismatic leaders will not appear in

---

2. Fox, *Journals*, 2:164.

3. Charisma: a special spiritual gift or power divinely conferred. A favor especially vouchsafed by God.

a church which has lost its connection with the prophetic tradition. You cannot graft prophetic leadership onto a community whose religion has become nonprophetic in character.

Second, the church can study its past and learn to covet the charismatic gift. The prophet is not gifted with some freakish hypersensitivity that takes possession of him and inhabits him sporadically in a way that is unrelated to his whole personality. He is a conscious chooser of the way of obedience. The prophet's obedience is a part of the obedience that is the foundation of the church's life and the prophetic gift is imparted for the benefit of the church as a whole. It is something that neither the church nor the individual can create but which can and should be expected.

There is a unique relationship between the charismatic leader and the church community. The minister, while receiving his gift from God and exercising it under the direction of the Head of the church, is nevertheless answerable to the whole church in so far as the church looks to its head for guidance. The prophetic minister does not announce his own gift or make claims for himself. If he is faithful in exercising his gift, then the church confirms it by formal recognition. But before he is thus recognized he may need loving counsel and encouragement. After the general recognition of his gift the church still has a responsibility to counsel and guide the maturing minister. He in turn submits to the church's judgment his leading to service in the ministry.

The Quaker minister is not a freewheeling, unattached preacher. His service is performed with the full knowledge and support of the church, and its end is to build up and edify the church. The church participates in, rather than controls, the ministry. The traveling minister carries with him a written expression of the concurrence of the church in his call to service, and when he returns from his travels, he brings the written endorsements of the groups in which he has labored. The church helps the minister largely through the work of a few of its members, called elders, who, while not themselves engaged in vocal ministry, are gifted with a sense of the nature and right exercise of ministry. These persons share with ministers the responsibility for holding meetings for worship and show a loving, watchful care for the immature or undisciplined minister. This service is also a charismatic gift, and without it the prophetic minister is a lonely soul subject to special temptations and neuroses. The minister needs and should always have the spiritual support of the whole church and the advice of gifted elders.

Prophetic leadership is often mistakenly equated with unpaid leadership. Prophetic ministry is nonclerical and nonprofessional, and it does not seek paid offices in the church which appear "vacant." But just as the church is concerned to uphold the minister with spiritual support, so also it must consider in what ways his labors can be strengthened by material support. The ministry is not territorial or parochial. It is a service to the whole church, and should therefore be supported by the whole church, insofar as the church may have become concerned in any particular service. A full-time paid minister of a particular congregation is not an outgrowth of the prophetic conception of Christian community but is derived from institutional Christianity. The minister should not be encouraged to look to the church as his sole means of support. Prophetic ministry is not a trade or profession. Its validity rests on the degree to which the minister is answerable to the speaking God. Service in the prophetic ministry is always a particular term of service in particular places to particular groups. It must be accepted regardless of available financial resources. But any meeting that has expressed its unity with a prospective service ought to be concerned that it is not hindered for lack of material support. The true church is a missionary church, and the financial resources of the church should be available for the support of the laborer in God's vineyard. However, this should be kept rigidly distinct from any system of a salaried hierarchy and from the establishment of permanent "livings" that must be kept filled, and which are sought after as a maintenance.

Ministers who receive material support ought never to be viewed as hired leaders whose continued support depends on carrying out a work schedule imposed by the church. When the church helps to support its ministers, it is under great necessity not to let its right hand know what its left hand is doing. The church is not paying for services rendered. Its financial support is a form of participation in a service which is initiated, not by the church, but by God and Christ. The minister does not perform his service on the basis of a contract with the church but on a basis of obedience to God. The prophetic minister is not a replaceable hired functionary. To share in his service is the church's privilege. In doing so it does not become the minister's employer and he does not become the church's employee.

The prophetic minister's service is unique. He labors in a community that is a spiritual organism directed and sustained by the power of God, and he is called to act of service by the Head of the church. He does not occupy a place in a hierarchical pyramid with bishops above him and laity below him. He brings fresh vision to his fellow disciples and a sense of spiritual direction, but he does not direct or control by any other means than the convincing power of Truth. He does not speak for the church as its official representative and does not correspond at all to the clergy of the institutional church. He is a member of a congregation, but they are not "his" congregation. There may be other ministers in the same congregation and his field of service may lie outside the limits of the congregation where he is a member. He is the recipient of no special deference or titles of respect and honor. He does not automatically represent the church in interfaith or interdenominational gatherings, and when such representatives are chosen, he is not deemed to have any special qualification by virtue of his calling and service in the ministry. He is not an indispensable participant in meetings for marriages and funerals.

Moreover, although the minister appears in a more public way than the recipients of other spiritual gifts, his is only one among many and his service should be integrated with those of others. If there is any special quality connected with his service it lies in the greatness of his responsibility, for it is through the exercise of his gift that the church can be called back to her true foundation when she has gone astray. If the church has wandered and strayed, it is from Christ and it is the task of the ministry to call people back to him. A church which is not served by such a ministry cannot fulfill the vision of the new covenant community.

6

The Preacher and Preaching

WALTER KLAASSEN

There is a growing recognition among Mennonite historians and scholars that despite all the exciting discoveries in sixteenth-century Anabaptist history and theology we cannot adopt the slogan "Back to the Sixteenth Century." But one does not need to work long in the field of Anabaptist research before one discovers that it is so easy, so deceptively easy to come under the spell of the sixteenth century—the time when faith was a new discovery, and when it was being tempered in the fiery forge of persecution and hammered out on the anvil of oppression. It was a time when men like ourselves, young men just out of college, were gripped by the Spirit of God in a thoroughly New Testament manner, causing them to "Speak Forth" fearlessly about what they knew to be God's truth. Oh, what lives they lived! How valiant was their defense of the faith, how heroic their manner as they yielded their bodies to be tortured and burned; these things sear deeply into the soul, and suddenly one realizes that they had a power of persuasion that by no means exhausted itself in the sixteenth century. "They being dead yet speak!" They convinced me when no living man could have done it. Theirs is a mighty attraction that draws one like a great magnet, and one almost naturally responds by saying, "We must get back to the sixteenth century." There is the pure fountainhead of Anabaptist genius. Let us bypass the intervening centuries of Anabaptist-Mennonite life during which time the dead leaves of conformity and the silt of ignorance have clogged up the clear stream so that it muddles along sluggishly, with little to commend it to the searcher for a revitalizing draught. Let us therefore get back to the beginning and start over again.

PART I: ON PASTORAL MINISTRY

"Zeal for the faith is good but this is zeal without knowledge." Alas, we cannot get back to the sixteenth century and thus recapture what Grebel, Sattler, Denck, Hut, and Marpeck had, any more than we can get back to the formative age of democracy in the eighteenth century. The purpose of God moves forward into the future, not backward into the past. "They must upward still and onward, who would keep abreast of truth." This, of course, does not mean that we disregard the past. In fact, many of the bricks and stones used by generations before us may be dug out from the ruins of the past and integrated into the building that we are now erecting.

I want, in this paper, to pick up some of those bricks and stones and examine them to see whether they may be used again. I believe firmly that the field of Anabaptist history and theology is not merely a happy hunting ground for suitable MA and PhD theses, but that its findings can also shed valuable light on problems which we face today. It is of the nature of the Christian witness that it must constantly be rethought and reinterpreted. To say, as some do in the interests of ecumenical understanding, that the old battles have lost their significance and ought no longer to be fought is therefore to give evidence of a certain misunderstanding of the nature of the Christian witness.

My concern here is with the ministry of our churches, and so I want to say something about the preacher, his call, and the function of preaching, allowing what the Anabaptists had to say about this to shed some light on the question. If I now venture to say a few things about the state of the ministry today, I am merely outlining my own observations and the conclusions to which I have come as a result and am in no sense putting this forward as verified fact. In any case we are dealing here with something in which definite classified information is next to impossible to obtain. Moreover, although my observations and personal experience have been outside the Mennonite tradition, I believe that we represent no significant exception to what I am going to say.

The Christian ministry today is in the eyes of most people a profession, like medicine or law or teaching. To be sure the minister is still considered to be a special person in the community. Soon after his arrival he becomes known as the Rev. and is regarded as the sort of man who has quite a considerable amount of spare time, in addition to having a college education, all of which he may fruitfully bring to bear on community projects. And so, he is elected chairman of the committee in charge of building a new skating arena. Again, because he has a college degree and perhaps even two or three degrees, and because of course he is a man interested in the welfare of the community in which he serves, he is put in charge of the committee for the United Fund Appeal that goes out every autumn. He is also the man, because of his undoubted humanitarian concern, who is honored with the position of local probation officer. Again, and this may be more applicable in Canada and Britain than in the United States, because a minister is concerned with social problems he is sometimes asked to run for election in provincial and municipal elections. I can think of several cases, one of which came to my attention only last summer and another just a few weeks ago. Further underlining his professional status is the fact that he frequently gets professional courtesies, especially from physicians when it comes to paying the bills for his family's illness.

Within the framework of the congregation or parish which he serves the matter is not much different. He is regarded as an expert on all phases of church activity and administration, and therefore it is best to leave many of the administrative matters in his hands. Not only is he regarded as competent, but it is considered to be his duty since that is why he is "hired," and I use that word advisedly. The congregation just does not have time to look after these things.

The minister is therefore largely looked upon as a dedicated and usually capable administrative officer who has some affinity with religious matters since he is the "employee" of the congregation or church which he serves. This religious coloring which the minister has makes him, on the whole, a reliable force for good in the community, but other than that it is incidental. Frequently it is indulgently shrugged off as an occupational eccentricity. The view that the Christian minister is in any way a unique phenomenon in society would be rejected not only by the civic community but in many cases also by the church or congregation. This means that the Christian minister often holds no more respect in either community or church than any other professional person.

All this is said as description, and at least as far as the civic community is concerned one cannot either condemn or commend this attitude toward the Christian minister. Where the congregation or church is concerned one can of course sit in judgment, saying that it ought to know better, but even there we shall reserve judgment. The big problem here is not that the community and church regard the minister as an ordained executive but that the ministry itself has come to regard its function largely in the terms described above. I have for years been concerned about it (beginning as a young man of twenty-one looking at the ministry as my life work) and have in many places talked with minsters about it. Whenever I began to say something about the priorities of the minister in terms of function I have been met with an indulgent and slightly impatient smile, pity for my inexperience and idealism, and the assurance that once I get into the ministry I will no longer have any choice about priorities. The practical situation will dictate to me my priorities. There was almost invariably a tacit acceptance of the function of the minister as I have described it. I admit that I am inexperienced, and I know even from the little experience I have had in the active ministry that the battle is hard and that it is discouraging and frustrating at many points. But I also know without the shadow of a doubt that such acceptance of an almost completely secularized function for the minister's main concern is compromise and disobedience to the God who in Jesus Christ calls men into his service.

On this view of the ministry, preaching can have little meaning beyond trying to give the congregation little moral shots in the arm on the analogy of the manager's words at weekly staff meetings, which for the most part are regarded as good advice, but which, because of the world in which we live, are really impractical. On such a view of the ministry *Seelsorge* or the care of souls also has little significance, and this is evident from the fact that many ministers no longer regard extended visitation as desirable or necessary. On such an approach to the function of the ministry the sacraments lose their deep theological meaning and become a part of the normal routine of the institution. A deacon came to me one day in a small Baptist church of which I was the minister and announced, "It is about time we had some more baptisms around here!" Strongly underlining this depreciation of preaching is the regular spate of books about the techniques of preaching but only a few books, praise God there are some, dealing with the basic facts; that which justifies the minister's existence in the first place; the theology of the ministry; the theology of the minister's message; the theology of the sacraments. There is a fantastic amount of stuff put out under titles like: "70 Snappy Sermon Starters" or "Prepared Preaching Précis for Busy Preachers." All this gives the impression that although preaching is unfortunately a part of our business as ministers, let's make it as easy as we can with the minimum of time consumption. I admit that I have drawn a very dismal and disheartening picture. Of course, there are exceptions to this, but they are too few. The "organization man" evil has invaded the Christian ministry along with the rest of society.

All of this amounts to betrayal of the trust that God has given us. It means that as ministers we are in many cases doing the wrong things and the priorities are neglected in favor of demands that make more noise and that are, all in all, easier to satisfy. Now it has taken me a long time to get around to the Anabaptists, but I have arrived. They had some notions about the call of the preacher and the function of preaching which we would do well to consider seriously.

First of all, I want to say something about secularization and professionalism as, in their view, it affected the ministry. Let us not think that secularism is a new thing. It has perhaps never before come in quite the form in which we know it today, but it is as old as religion. In the sixteenth century it assumed a shape peculiar to its age. Church and state were one, and as is invariably the case where such a union exists, the church descends to the level of the state rather than drawing the state up to its own higher level. This inevitably involves the clergy who, in a secularized church, tend to become lackeys of the state. During the Reformation many of the bishops and archbishops were also secular princes, and those on the lower hierarchical levels in many cases knew practically nothing about their religious functions as priests. The mere fact that many of them became Protestant clerics when they forsook Romanism did not make them capable of performing the duties of an evangelical pastor. They enjoyed the protection and support of the state in which they were employed. They preached the Reformation doctrine of justification by faith, but frequently, along with their congregations, they continued the undisciplined and irreligious lives they had lived before.

Furthermore, the division between clergy and laity was carefully observed. Zwingli and his fellow reformers were at first inclined to minimize this, emphasizing that every person had direct access to the means of grace, and that the clergy had no prerogatives in this respect. After their strife with the Anabaptist separatists, however, they tended to retreat from this position. At the Bern Disputation they made it clear that it was the business of the laity to look after family and profession, and to leave religious enquiry and teaching to the clergy who were educated for that purpose. Thus, the line between clergy and laity was again clearly drawn as a security measure.

The Anabaptists protested vigorously against this secular professionalism. Such preachers, they said, ought not to be listened to because their manner of living makes it impossible that they could preach the gospel as

God desires it. In Augsburg the Anabaptists complained that the evil lives of the preachers prevented their words from doing any good. The most bitter complaints come from the Hut tradition. Because the clergy have not been called by God through the fellowship of believers and nevertheless claim to be Christ's representatives, they must be considered to be false prophets, and therefore they ought not to be listened to. They lack the Holy Spirit, says Marpeck, and therefore they cannot be distinguished from anyone else who does not know God. The problem is that because they are in positions of religious authority their words are considered to be the words of God. Since however, they are not inspired by the Spirit of God, their words are in fact ridden with error, and those who listen to them are led astray. Men such as this can by no means be considered true ministers of Christ. To Anabaptists it seemed as though they were in the ministry merely to make a living and not because of an encounter with the living God.

The message of this Anabaptist protest is clear. Although the situation is different today, the dangers of secularism and professionalism are manifest. Men who take a professional rather than a vocational view of the ministry cannot be considered true ministers of Christ in the biblical sense. The same is true of those who allow the pressures of modern living to force them into a secularized view of their ministry. There are few men who deliberately allow this to happen, but it happens, nevertheless. Only a clear vision of the function of the minister will prevent this and this vision must be nurtured constantly by communion with God, lest it fade and something less compelling take its place.

Secondly, I would like to summarize the evidence for what the Anabaptists believed about the call to the Christian ministry. It was on this matter of the ministry that they were attacked again and again by their inquisitors. By maintaining that their ministry was not valid the clergy of the established churches attempted to convince the Anabaptists that they had no right to preach. They were repeatedly told that they had not been commissioned and ordained by the church in an orderly manner, and since the church had not legitimized them, they had no right to preach. This charge was summarily rejected by the Anabaptists. Numerous references in the Swiss *Tauferakten* testify to a conviction of being sent by God to preach, and they repudiated any suggestion that they had undertaken to do this of their own initiative. A simple Swiss Brother said that his Creator had called him to proclaim his word. Gabriel Giger of St. Gallen explained it by saying, "he was not his own, and would do that commanded him by God."

George Blaurock was especially conscious of being chosen and called by God. On one occasion he ascended the pulpit of the little church at Hinwil and said, "I am an emissary of the Father, sent to preach the Word of God." At a disputation in Zofingen in 1523 Swiss Brethren insisted again that they had been sent by Christ and not from any authority of their own. Hans Denk also emphasized that a man must be called by God to preach, and that one who is not so called has no right to preach. Again, we find this in the Hut tradition. The preacher, they said, must be called by God. Gabriel Weinberger wrote in a letter to the council of Regensburg in 1540, that he knew and had experienced that congregations and true churches of Christ did not elect a preacher and servant of the gospel unless he was first called by God and driven by the Holy Spirit. Only the man whom God has called has the right to preach.

But this is only one side of their emphasis. The other side is that although a man is called of God that call must be examined and weighed and confirmed by the church. This was insisted on at length in the great disputation between Swiss Brethren and Zwinglians at Berne in 1538. The result of this insistence was that the state church clergy set about to prove that the church about which the Swiss Brethren spoke was no true church at all, seeking in this way to invalidate the Anabaptist ministry. The clearest statements on the function of the church in calling the minister come to us from the Hut tradition. Here again we find the repeated emphatic assertion that their preachers are properly called and ordained. The initial sending is by God, but God makes known his will in sending his servants through the fellowship of the church which then confirms the call of God. This confirmation of the call is almost invariably mentioned in the same breath with the assertion of the Divine Call. Ambrosius Spitlmayr said that he had been sent by his heavenly Father through Hans Hut, his instrument. Hans Raiffer, a Hutterite missionary insisted that "he had not installed himself in the office, but God and His Spirit in the congregation. For as He sent His beloved Son and the Son His apostles into all the world, so He still sends His servants through His spirit that they . . . preach the word of God."

God therefore calls his servants to his service through the fellowship of believers, the church. But it is God that takes the first step in calling his servants. The one thing that is so tremendously impressive about those sixteenth-century preachers is their burning conviction that they were chosen and sent by the God who was the Creator of all things; the God who had long ago called Abraham and Moses and David and Isaiah and

Jeremiah and the apostles. This same God, who had in by-gone ages chosen for himself men, weak, human, erring men, had done so once again, but this time he had chosen them. His call had once again been heard in the midst of human affairs, and when God Almighty calls, what can man do but listen? He had chosen them, weak and sinful though they were, incapable as they were. They were overwhelmed with the wonder and mystery of it, they marveled at the God who once again chose the weak to confound the strong. They accepted the challenge and said, "Here I am, send me." And they went out with the conviction that they were partners with God; that they had a living and a vital part to play in the great purpose of the God who had revealed himself in Jesus Christ.

I suppose we can justifiably say that the above picture of the call of a minister still obtains with us and that is good. We still say that God calls a man through the fellowship of the church. But how big is our view of the ministry? Do we still know the excitement and the wonder of being called to serve God? Have we this same overwhelming conviction of being co-workers with God in a purpose of cosmic proportions? Are we conscious of the fact that we do stand in the very succession of the apostles and that we are thus the very representatives of the Holy God? Do we believe, that in our little churches in town or country, with all the attendant discouragements, that we are actually on business for the Lord of all the Earth? Do we amid the almost unbelievably complex program of activity in our large city churches, manage to keep this overwhelming conviction of being called by the Great God to this work uppermost in heart and mind? We say, of course, that we do. It is the right thing to say; what else could we say? But are we convinced without the shadow of a doubt, so convinced that there is nothing of which we are more certain? This is terribly important, for the crisis we face in the world today is infinitely greater than that faced by our Anabaptist forebearers. Unless these convictions again grip us so that we become slaves of Christ we will perish with our world.

There is no doubt whatever that the Anabaptists believed preaching to be one of the priorities of those who were called by God through the church. It is interesting and instructive for us to notice, thirdly, what they considered preaching to be. It is stated in clear and unambiguous terms. Preaching, they taught, is the proclamation of the good news of forgiveness and salvation in Christ, the oral witness to the great acts of God in Jesus Christ. Along with the Scriptures, preaching is the means by which God makes his Divine will known to mankind, and in those days preaching was a good deal more important than it is now simply because many folk could not read the Bible but they could hear the preacher. By preaching then, men are persuaded to repent, accept God's offer of salvation by faith, which acceptance is then followed by baptism. All this means nothing more or less than that they believed that preaching, human preaching, becomes the church. This is stated in so many words by Marpeck in 1542: "It is undeniable and irrefutable that this is the first, through which the church came into being and still does, namely the proclamation of the Holy Gospel of Christ." Because of this they were always at pains to emphasize that the primary place in the order of the church belongs to the preaching of God's word. The sacraments follow after preaching; baptism when a man believes the Word, and the Lord's Supper when, through faith in baptism, he has become a member of the church of Christ. Without the external witness of preaching there could be no church at all.

Naturally the preaching about which they speak is not a human effort. It is rightly done by men filled with the Holy Spirit, having themselves experienced the new birth. "It is necessary," says P. Rideman in his famous "Confession," "that the builders who would build on this foundation must first be planted and rooted in Him, have grasped His full nature, mind, and character." A true preacher must be taught of God for he has a divine and not a human task. The human response to the preacher in terms of faith is a miracle wrought by the Holy Spirit of God who takes the preacher's words, fructifies them, and by them as through a seed, produces the new birth. Preaching, to them, was also the medium for the proclamation of the will of God for his redeemed people, and thus the means for building up the church.

So much of the preaching that we hear nowadays from the pulpits of our land would not measure up to those high ideals expressed above. What the Anabaptists had as a theology of preaching was not man-centered but God-centered. God does the work; men are but the instruments. And yet it was to them a marvel that God should choose this very human medium for so great a purpose. This made them very conscious of being in the presence of God when they were preaching. They realized that they were responsible to God for what they said. Again, we would do well to emulate them. For they were right in their evaluation of the function of preaching in the purpose of God. It is first and foremost the proclamation of the *kerygma*, the recital of the great acts which God did in time, in the man Jesus Christ. These are the things that are important, because they have happened and through them, we have come into a new age. We live in the age of the peace of God, in the year of our Lord. God has made his peace with the world, but the world still does not know it. Our business as preachers is to preach about the death and resurrection and ascension of Christ in all its variations. And when this message has been proclaimed, we call men to repentance toward God and faith in the Lord Jesus Christ. This is our primary duty, our first responsibility, and all other demands must yield to this one—it makes no difference what they are. It means that we must immerse ourselves in these truths, think about them constantly, and read widely in the things written about them. And this takes time, it takes quietness. If we compromise on this issue, we are betraying our trust both to God and to the human race, that part of the human race that we of all others have been called to serve. This is terribly serious business. St. Paul knew how serious it was, for he considered it a possibility that he could in the end be a castaway because of betrayal. The Anabaptist preachers were also very much aware of this; their prayers testify to an overwhelming sense of responsibility. Among the pressures to which the ministry today is subject you will yourselves have to make the choice, but remember that since you have been called by God, your standard of priority can never be one set by men, no matter who they are, but always and only by God, to whom you are answerable.

There is one other thing that deserves mention here. The Anabaptists always insist that the test of true preaching is whether it is Scriptural or not. Preaching and the Scriptures are inseparably connected in their thinking. The Scriptures are the norm which God has been pleased to give man whereby he can test his faith and his conduct. They recognized that the danger of subjectivism in preaching is great, and the only way to control it is with the norm of Scripture. Hubmaier said in one of his lucid writings, "God does not want interpretation of the Scriptures, nor will He accept fabrication composed by the human will. But we are to do nothing else than to teach the wholesome words of Christ." This may sound suspicious but let me assure you that by interpretation they did not mean exegesis and exposition; they meant the introduction of human judgments. For this, they believed, there was no room in preaching, since preaching concerned itself with divine truth, and human judgment would certainly introduce error. If a man stay with the truth as it has been revealed by God, wrote Hans Denck, a preacher need never fear that his message will be false, "for he who has the truth has a spring that he will nevermore be able to exhaust, so that he does not need to resort to the fictions and dreams of his own heart. Woe to him who does not take time to draw from it."

In answer to student complaints about the difficulty of finding preaching material, the principal of my seminary said in class one day, "Have you boys ever tried preaching from the Bible? It's the most exhaustive book of texts there is." And so it is. The Bible contains the message on which the redemption and salvation of the human race depends. This is important and significant enough that those of us who believe we have been called by God, should devote a major portion of our time to becoming familiar with its contents, not merely to know the words and the sequence and all the rest of it, but to learn from its chapters the deeper and more profound meaning of the will of God for us and for others, and to be refreshed by the pure winds of the Spirit that blow from its pages. There is no substitute for this, as the Anabaptist preachers insisted again and again. Commentaries and theologies and philosophies are necessary, but they can never replace the study of the Scriptures. Certainly, this is an inexhaustible spring, and again: Woe to him who does not take time to draw from it! This is as true today as ever it was.

7

Discipleship and Church Order

A Review and Discussion

WILLIAM KLASSEN

Certain New Testament scholars are addressing themselves directly to the issues facing the twentieth-century church. This is particularly true of Eduard Schweizer who has distinguished himself as a pastor and also as a New Testament theologian. The two books listed at the end of this article will be discussed here in an attempt to appraise the readers of *Concern* of the position taken, as well as in general terms to evaluate their reliability. No attempt will be made to enter into the critical discussion of the finer points of the argument.

The work of men like Dietrich Bonhoeffer (strangely never referred to by Schweizer) has emphasized particularly the place that discipleship has in the Gospel of Matthew and in the teachings of Jesus. In our tradition through the dedicated work of H. S. Bender, the theme of discipleship has often been stressed as the center of the Anabaptist vision. The idea of discipleship has formed a focal center of the Christian life for many of us.

Another theme that has repeatedly been struck in the recent theological discussion is the theme of the lordship of Christ. Particularly Oscar Cullmann has stressed the centrality of the lordship of Christ in the confessions of the early church. As in our day other lords have clamored for attention and devotion the theme of the lordship of Christ has risen from the biblical documents with peculiar urgency and vitality. What was always latent in them became extremely relevant to the church as it sought to deflect the challenge of other lords.

Strange as it may seem, however, Schweizer is the first in his book, *Lordship and Discipleship*, to bring together these two dominant strands in the biblical view of the Christian life. He does so by devoting his first chapter to the theme of following Jesus. He begins with the apt illustration of the child caught in a heavy snowfall who must make his way home. The father comes to break the way open through the snowdrifts for him, and the child follows step by step in the footsteps of the father, yet in an entirely different manner. If the father wanted to be just an "example" then the child would have to make his own way ten yards away from the father and merely imitate the manner in which the latter makes his way. If the father wanted to act "vicariously" for the child, in the strict sense of the word, then the child would stay with grandmother and think: "Father's going home in my stead."

From this illustration it becomes obvious that Schweizer is attempting to strike a middle road between the two positions taken with respect to the relevance of Christ's life for the Christian. The illustration is to serve only as a picture but "it raises the question for the New Testament whether early Christianity has not regarded Jesus Christ as in the same sense 'going on before' and, if so, what this meant to those who so understood him."[1] He notes that the word "to follow" is used in the New Testament, with one exception, exclusively of the relationship to the earthly Jesus.

The idea of following a deity is common among the Greeks but only in a sense that men would become like the deity. For the rabbis to follow God meant to imitate his virtues. The radical aspect of the New Testament called discipleship is stressed by Schweizer particularly in the saying of Jesus "If any man would come after me, let him deny himself, take up his cross, and follow me." Schweizer notes that there is no real parallel to this saying in antiquity[2] and that in Hellenistic stories the carrying of a cross was always regarded as a disgrace.

In chapter 2 Schweizer deals with "the suffering and exalted righteous one" in Judaism and he observes that for the mind of late Judaism, religion is obedience. He quotes from Bousset "Humble, servile submission of the human will to God's almighty, inscrutable will, acting according to his commandments, comprehensible or incomprehensible, at every moment of life—this is piety."[3] In addition to this, special emphasis is placed

---

1. Schweizer, *Lordship and Discipleship*, 11.
2. Schweizer, *Lordship and Discipleship*, 17.
3. Schweizer, *Lordship and Discipleship*, 24.

on suffering and the atoning power which this suffering has. Thoughts of the exaltation of the righteous one were also a living issue. As a result of suffering, God will exalt. Such suffering can have a vicarious effect already in pre-New Testament Judaism.

Chapter 3 deals with the understanding of Jesus in the early church in terms of the suffering and exalted righteous one. Here one sees the conviction of the early Christians that in Jesus's suffering and exaltation the hope for the righteous one in Judaism has been fulfilled. Chapter 4 elaborates this theme in the evidence that the church saw in Jesus the representative of the true Israel. Similarly, they saw in Jesus an exalted and suffering servant of God (chapter 5).

Schweizer's method allows the variety of New Testament concepts to come to full expression, as well as noting their essential unity. In the book on discipleship the tenth chapter deals with the unity among them while the eleventh chapter deals with the varieties. The twelfth chapter has the theme of the translation of the message for the Hellenistic church while the thirteenth chapter deals with the preservation of the original message in the translation. Schweizer's keen interest in communicating the gospel to modern man comes to expression also in these chapters. He makes the rather telling observation that the Jew is interested in forgiveness of sins and in his ability to stand before a righteous God while the Greek is troubled by the question of fate. His concern is to find meaning in an impersonal universe. In masterful strokes Schweizer portrays the shifts of emphases within the New Testament itself where the message is directed to Greeks and to Jews. The application is obvious. In our own day, these two problems continue to haunt people and our presentation of the message should offer a solution for both problems in relevant terms.

For those who look for specific indications of how discipleship spells itself out in actual life, a reading of this book will prove disappointing. For those, however, who are interested in a solid documentation of the essential union of the themes of lordship of Christ and discipleship within the New Testament, a reading of this book will prove immensely rewarding. If the author's somewhat skeptical attitude toward the genuineness of certain sayings of Jesus can be overlooked, this book should be helpful in our own present search to give discipleship more theological and biblical depth.

The second book deals with the question of church order. Here, again, Schweizer sees the New Testament from the standpoint of gospel. It is not to be seen as a new law which must be imitated in the area of church order;

on the other hand, we cannot ignore it. The battle of the confessing church in Germany has shown that a church order which is not oriented biblically is subject to the whims of the state.[4] Thus, Schweizer is not interested in any "mere repetition of the New Testament formulas or rules" because they do not guarantee the purity of the church any more than does a continuous development with a definite tradition. Church history helps in the task of the translation of the New Testament church order for our own time, but it is not to be seen as a second source of revelation. Schweizer's basic concern is to listen to the New Testament in an evangelic way.

This listening is not naive because Schweizer brings to this study all the technical tools at his disposal as well as the results of modern form criticism. Thus, he calls into question Jesus's use of the term "church" and his intent to train disciples. At a number of points, it seems that he is overly critical, but essentially, the argument of his book is not affected by this position. Certain treatments like that of R. Newton Flew and Theophil Spoerri are ignored.

The main outline of the book consists of a treatment of the conception of the church which Jesus held (fourteen pages) and the conception held by the primitive church as it is reflected in the early church in Jerusalem, the church of Matthew, the church of Luke, and that presupposed in the pastoral epistles. Paul's conception and its influence is then dealt with as well as that of John and the Apostolic Fathers. By speaking of the influence of Paul's conception of the church and that of John, he can deal with the Pauline material as well as those writings obviously influenced by Paul or those which share Paul's concept of the church. By bringing into the comparative study the concept of the church held by the Apostolic Fathers, the contrast between the canonical material and the post-canonical material comes into sharp focus.

The second major section of the book deals with the unity of the New Testament church concept. Here such matters as office, charismatic services, priesthood of all believers, order as manifestation of the Spirit, ordination, etc., are dealt with.

It is not possible to take up each one of these subjects, all of them important and significant in themselves. Several illustrations must suffice to indicate the difference that Schweizer finds between the second-century church concept and that found in the canonical materials. Modern churches tend to make decisions by the use of the ballot. Presumably, if 51 percent

---

4. Schweizer, *Gemeinde und Gemeindeordnung*, 8.

of the people vote for something, this action has to be carried out. Over against this, Schweizer observes that the New Testament knows nothing of decision by majority vote[5] and that such is, in fact, in direct contradiction to the New Testament concept of the church. This could have been illustrated even more with references to the stress in Acts on unanimity, as well as the often-ignored fact that the ballot was available to the early church. Was it perhaps used in the election of Matthias? The Greek of Acts 1:26 leaves the possibility open. Too often we assume that the modern methods of democracy were not available to the early church, inferring that had they known about ballots they would have used them. But this is to misunderstand the historical situation in which the church found itself. The absence of the ballot in the New Testament church order is a powerful argument because this is not by chance. Indeed, as Schweizer shows, the principle of majority rule appears in the church as early as 1 Clement (about the year ninety-six in Rome). One has in 1 Clement the clear desire for a guaranteed tradition and a guaranteed order. Herein lies the great contrast between Paul and 1 Clement. The spirit takes an orderly direction in Paul as well, but order is never meant to guarantee the power of the Spirit.

There are a number of other points on which Schweizer is equally relevant. It is to be hoped that the issues he presents will be tested by the evidence in the New Testament, not simply rejected because they call into question much of our traditional church machinery.

In many respects his book on church order has much to say to us because, as a rule, Mennonites have allowed the institutional church to remain immune to the voice of the New Testament on matters of church order. One could mention the evidence he supplies on the administration of the sacraments which in the New Testament required no ordination— to say nothing of a double ordination! In most Mennonite groups a duly ordained man is not permitted to administer the sacraments until he has been ordained an elder or bishop. How this radical departure from both the New Testament and our Anabaptist beginnings has become so inflexibly a part of church order is a mystery. In our present-day church structure this is the highest status to which one can achieve while Paul and the other apostles seem to have had little or no interest in the administration of the sacraments. We have assumed that we can distinguish between the essence and the form of the church and (somewhat naively) assumed that we have the essence, irrespective of the form that it takes. Obviously, our ancestors

---

5. Schweizer, *Gemeinde und Gemeindeordnung*, 192.

rejected such a spiritualizing interpretation, and wrestled seriously with church order. In fact, one might even say that at the basis of the rift between the Reformation and Anabaptists lay the question of church order in the deeper theological sense.

It is not only the local church, our growing conference structure, but also, and particularly, our institutions which should pay heed to books like Schweizer's. For in our institutions, we have distinguished between spiritual gift and office to such an extent that mandatory retirement policies, seniority, rank, status, have eclipsed not only natural talent, but certainly charismatic gifts. The question of charismatic gifts is seldom asked, and because of this, we are entitled to raise the question whether God's will is done in our institutions to the extent that we are sometimes led to believe. Institutions have at times abdicated positions of leadership because of the public relations aspect. This certainly is to deny a very basic part of the biblical concept of the church. Wherever a board or an institution whose role has been defined as that of a servant of the church refuses to assume the responsibilities of leadership, irrespective of the cost, it has lost the biblical conception of leadership and has yielded to modern political theory. It is on these levels that Schweizer has much to say to us.

In all three areas, the local church, the denominational structure, and the institutions, there is the constant danger that the machinery substitute for the openness of Christian encounter assumed as a gift of the Spirit on every page of the New Testament. It is much simpler to live by the law than it is to live by the gospel and where self-interest displaces the interest of Christ it is better to have rules of tenure, advancement, etc., than to allow these decisions to be made by authoritarian administrators. But the basic question of the effectiveness of one's service to Christ is seldom asked and the prophetic is stifled while the personal welfare of an individual as a part of the body of Christ is forgotten in the pursuit for the welfare of an institution or a program. There is no doubt that often our portrait of a church administrator has been entirely pagan and other denominations were better than we because they did not pretend to make the Bible apply to this area of life. Unless we develop a consistent philosophy on this level much respect for our heritage will be lost.

Lest it be assumed that administrators, boards, and institutions bear all the responsibility in this area, it should be observed that Schweizer's thesis judges most severely those of us who in the local congregation have failed to wrestle seriously with the process of decision-making, and other aspects of church order. How easy it is even in a small congregation to resort to Roberts Rules of Order and for the congregational meeting to become a place where business is merely acted upon in a perfunctory manner—where building plans and finances take the place of the real growth of the Christian church defined in terms of the increasing relevance of Christ for every area of life!

Even a limited amount of experience in a local church or an institution convinces us that much that Schweizer has to say on this subject is genuinely evangelical in that it convicts us all of sin. However, the gospel also offers us hope that where we are willing to listen to the sovereign voice of the Spirit, there new life will burst forth. It will have forms; forms that will often displace older ones, but these forms will always be means of serving Christ and as such must always submit to his Lordship.

We should be extremely grateful to Professor Schweizer for showing us in these books that the Lordship of Christ and Discipleship are related essentially to each other, and that church order cannot be separated from the nature of the church. Speaking to us from his own background and experience as pastor and teacher but above all as a devoted student of the New Testament what he tells us is extremely relevant for us. We should listen even when we must disagree on specific points of interpretation. There is enough here that convicts us all of unfaithfulness to the gospel.

There is a warning in this book finally about the one pastor system which is being rather unreflectively advocated in a number of Mennonite groups. When such a warning comes not from reactionaries within our own group but from men like Eduard Schweizer and Georg Eichholz[6] coming from denominations with long experience with the one pastor system, we should learn both from history and the New Testament on this point. Something of a novel way is suggested by Schweizer elsewhere when he describes his own experience of working out a sermon by using a number of his theologically untrained men to meet with him and share their understanding of a given text. In this way much time was added to the preparation of a sermon, but it was time well spent.

To be sure it is not Schweizer's purpose to speak to all the practical concerns of the church of the twentieth century. Obliquely however these two works encompass the important fields of church order and ethics and in both areas speak with relevance and authority.

---

6. Eichholz, *Was heisst charismatische Gemeinde?*

8

New Presbyter Is Old Priest Writ Large

WALTER KLAASSEN

The priest or the magic man has been part of the human religious scene from the very beginning. Dealing with the unseen world of demons, occult powers, gods was a role that not just anyone could assume. It required learning skills of all kinds, and the lore of the past. And it was of the highest importance that those skills, and the craft of priesthood and magic, be learned precisely because often the efficacy of the rite or spell depended on a letter-perfect performance.

Since the presence of the priest was ubiquitous in ancient religion it is not surprising to find him also among the Hebrews and later the Jews. He is the man who gives oracles, who tells people what the will of God is. He is a man who stands between the people and God and performs those rituals by which the people are assured of Yahweh's graciousness and forgiveness. Among the Hebrews, however, although he occupies a special position, he is not the magician in the sense that he possesses a store of secrets not available to anyone else. He is himself a man like other men who himself needs the assurance of God's graciousness and forgiveness. Nor is it his function to stand as a buffer between Yahweh and people, for he is not a propitiator, in the sense that he has to placate or turn away, or make non-effective, the wrath of an insulted God. The conviction of Israel was that God himself had given the ritual of atonement. Lev 17:11: "I have given . . . you [the blood] upon the altar." It was nothing that the priest did that made the ritual effective; he was simply the mediary.

Instead of the fund of secret knowledge, which was in the care of the pagan priest, the Hebrew priest was the teacher of Israel who taught the successive generations the great thing God had done for them in the past. He was therefore not a man in the possession of powers to keep the remnants of primeval chaos from breaking out against people, but someone who constantly reminded them that the God who had worked in the past in the life of Israel could be depended upon to do it today and tomorrow. He was the man who called people to trust and confidence in their God.

When we move from Judaism to the early Christian church, we find the priest completely absent. The reason for this is perhaps expressed by the book of Hebrews: the early church believed that Jesus Christ was the last priest as well as the last sacrificial victim.

But it was not for long. For a variety of reasons, the priest emerged again and within the Christian church. The process is complicated, having its origin both in the Old Testament and in influences from paganism. The basic motive in its emergence, whatever the manner, was that men were not prepared to live by faith, for with the priest there came also the elements usually associated with the priest in paganism. It was extremely difficult to believe that the death of Jesus on the cross centuries ago could be effective for a person in the seventh century. How is it made real in the ninth century or the fifteenth? And the church responded by saying that it is made real, it is contemporized in that the sacrifice of Christ is constantly repeated in the body and blood of the Mass. And for a sacrifice you need a priest. Gradually there came to be added also that other element, namely the words, the formula, which could be spoken only by a priest who had been sacralized by the ceremony of ordination which eventually came to be known as a sacrament. And the words had to be said correctly and accompanied by the right actions in order to achieve the miracle of turning the bread and wine into the body and blood of Jesus, so that the authentic sacrifice could be made on the altar.

In the medieval church there was literally no way for a person to receive God's grace except through the priest. He held the key to God's treasury and his control was almost absolute. If he did not turn the key no one else could. Here we have a revival of the pagan forms of priesthood rather than the Hebrew, for the Hebrew learned to get along without the priest while remaining a genuinely faithful Hebrew. In medieval Christianity anyone cut off from the offices of the priest was cut off from salvation. It was a reversion from faith to proof. Here were concrete ways of ordering and ensuring man's contact with God; if one did the right things, performed the right acts, said the right words, the contact with the divine was assured.

God had become a prisoner of the church, even as long ago the Hebrews had sought to imprison him in their temple.

It meant, of course, that a vast gulf was therefore fixed between clergy (the priesthood) and the laity (the people). They lived on different levels of moral expectation; one could not expect of the "common" person the moral achievement of a priest. The priest was therefore really separated from his people since he stood in a different relationship to God than they did. And everyone, priest and people alike, accepted this as good and right.

The Protestant Reformation was in a way a revolt against this religious unbelief. Luther and Calvin and the radical reformers insisted with one voice that all men have free access to God, without a sacramental priest. They insisted that all Christians are priests and all Christians are lay people, to take the New Testament *kleros* and *laos* seriously. But we don't break out of the habits of millennia all at once, and this insistence of the reformers has, with few exceptions, not yet been taken seriously in the church in any widespread way.

In 1653 John Milton wrote a short poem of protest entitled "On the New Forcers of Conscience."[1] It was directed at the Long Parliament which was very tardy in bringing about church reforms for which the Puritans were pressing. It is in this poem that the line appears which is the title of this lecture: "New presbyter is but old priest writ large." Milton was saying that the Reformation had not made any difference where views of the priesthood were concerned. Only the name had been changed.

It is because that old and striking line is still true in considerable measure that we have a crisis in the ministry today. It is primarily for this reason, I believe, that large numbers of seminary graduates go into social work, teaching, and other professions. It is for this reason that we get articles like the one that appeared in the *Christian Century* under the title "The Parochial Syndrome."[2] And here I wish to say simply, lest I be misunderstood, that I am not handing out blame; I am, after all, in spite of the fact that I am not ordained, regarded by most people as a cleric and so I cannot exclude myself here. On the basis of what I see and what I experience and what I read I simply want to describe where we are on this. It is in the nature of a self-examination. I believe there can be no doubt that among Mennonites too we have the problem of the separation of the clergy and the laity. We too make the usual primitive demands of

1. Milton, *Complete Poems*, 144–45.
2. Davis, "Parochial Syndrome."

our "priest." He must be above the normal aberrations of living; he may not have the passions we have; we expect him to be paternalistic, blessing us from his elevated sanctity; we expect him to be holy for us; we expect him to have all the answers to all the questions of life, and we expect him to give us clear, unequivocal, authoritative answers to these questions. We force him into a role in which he, and his family, have great difficulty being human and leading a normal human life. It is no wonder that young men refuse to be pushed into that kind of situation, but at the same time the men who do go into the ministry and work under that cruel handicap have my honest admiration.

And yet it doesn't need to be that way, for the Protestant emphasis on the priesthood of all believers is still largely lying fallow. Even we who claim to have understood it even better than Luther and Calvin did, constantly forsake it for the priestly fleshpots of Egypt, for it means that we can relax in the life of faith and let the minister do the struggling.

What do we want to relax from? We want to relax from the business of being priests to each other. The priesthood of all believers does not mean simply that we are our own priests in our access to God; it means that we, each one of us, are priests to each other. It means that God has put us in charge of each other so that we will intercede to God for each other; that we will make ourselves responsible for the well-being of others around us. It is from this that we would like to relax and let someone whom we pay a salary do it. In a sense the word of Jesus comes to us in this case: "They bind heavy burdens, hard to bear, and lay them on men's shoulders; but they themselves will not move them with their finger." It is clear that from the beginning the church has required leaders, people of vision and of spirit who led out, and the need exists today too. And changing the structure of the church will probably require more leadership rather than less.

But that is not my concern now. My concern is that you and I must prove John Milton wrong in our day. For we must assert that there is a legitimate priesthood, but it is a priesthood without secrets, without magic, without any pretensions of being above or separate from other persons. To become such a priest is an act of faith. It means that we—if it is an office given to each one of us—follow in the footsteps of Jesus and live on behalf of others as Jesus did. It means that we are priests not only on behalf of our friends but also on behalf of those who reject us or who think themselves our enemies. It means literally bearing their sins by absorbing their fear and enmity and thereby liberating them from the load of sin. It means being priests to each other and all men in the humdrum existence of day-to-day life when it is so easy to forget our priestly vocation. Being a priest means to help others, Christians and non-Christians, on the way of obedience to Christ. Being a priest means to love other men and do all we can to bring them with us on the pilgrimage of faith. This is how we contemporize the work of Christ, not by sacrificing him again on the altar, but by identifying ourselves with him and bearing the cross. Only as Christ is incarnated in us today in our relations with others will men around us listen to his call and submit to his lordship. Our faith is that what we do in this caring, loving way for others is not in vain.

9

Theological Education for the Believers' Church

J. Lawrence Burkholder[1]

Professional Theological Education

Probably no realm of education has been more stereotyped during the past fifty years than theological education. It is a curious fact that despite the pluralism of American Christianity, and despite revolutionary cultural changes, all Protestant seminaries, if we exclude Bible schools, have adopted a relatively uniform pattern of theological education. Although many of our denominational seminaries were established in the nineteenth century for the purpose of defending and promoting particular theologies, it is noteworthy that all have seemed to agree upon what it takes to educate for the ministry. It has been agreed by Episcopalians, Presbyterians, Baptists, and now by Mennonites, that it takes precisely three years beyond college, no more, no less, for everyone, regardless of who he is, and whether he plans to minister to the hill folk of Kentucky or the matrons of Madison Avenue, and regardless of whether the church is conceived as a sacramental institution or a pilgrim fellowship. Furthermore, curricular developments have undergone the same changes in all seminaries with emphasis upon Christian education in the 1920s and 1930s, clinical psychology in the 1940s and 1950s, and social sciences in the 1960s. Significant differences lie only in the areas of doctrine and liturgy. Curriculums have been structured so much alike that one may assume that sensitivity to the immediate needs

---

1. This material was first presented in a series of lectures at the Associated Mennonite Seminaries, Elkhart, Indiana, in December 1967.

of particular churches has not been the dominant consideration. If each institution had molded its curriculum according to its concept of Christianity and according to the needs of its constituency, we would have in the United States an educational pluralism which I believe would be a sign of health in a pluralistic society. In America, theological education has fallen for a false structuralization. One is tempted to say that many schools have misconstrued formal requirements for excellence. Consequently, whether it is good education or poor education, it still takes precisely three years to get enough of it for any and all ministries!

Furthermore, theological education has had neither the wisdom nor the courage to carry out the implications of its own discoveries. For example, it is agreed generally that the conception of the ministry has changed. It has been agreed that the ministry belongs fundamentally to the laity. The point which Kraemer made in his epochal volume, *A Theology of the Laity*, is now standard doctrine.[2] Yet there have been few, if any, proposals for revolutionary changes in theological education in light of the discovery of the ministry of the laity. Changes have been largely verbal. With one or two exceptions, seminaries have continued as before to train men and women for "the ministry."

It seems to me that the time has come to break the stereotype. This is not to suggest that fragmentation is a good thing in itself. Furthermore, criticism of uniformism should not be interpreted as an un-ecumenical gesture. Rather, the time has come for all institutions to examine their purposes and their programs in order to come to terms with their traditions, the needs of their constituencies, and their peculiar places in theological education at large.

The Model

I plan to be so audacious and possibly so presumptuous as to present a model for theological education in the free church tradition with the Associated Mennonite Seminaries directly in mind. This model would attempt to express structurally the pivotal points of the Anabaptist-Mennonite tradition, while anticipating ecumenical developments in theological education. It would seek to express the implications of brotherhood, charismatic structure, and the nonprofessional ministry, while making a place for a redefined professional ministry. It would attempt to take a positive attitude toward

2. Kraemer, *Theology*.

youth mentality, including vocational uncertainty, identity crises, and alienation. It would seek to incorporate within a single community the reality of the church and the structures of the institution.

Where do we begin? I believe that it would be helpful to clarify first of all certain basic structural concepts. The model which I am about to propose involves education on three related levels. Level I is college education with special emphasis upon religion during the junior and senior years. Level II is seminary education designed especially for the nonprofessional ministries. Those who would complete two years on Level II may receive an academic degree, though the primary purpose of Level II would be to prepare men and women for "commissioning," which may occur before two years are completed. By commissioning we mean authorization by the school and the church to "preach and baptize" as nonprofessional ministers and missioners. Level III is training for the professional ministry in one of its many forms. Levels I and II are prerequisite for Level III. Level III leads to a professional degree. Level III is ecumenical in the sense that it involves residence somewhere other than at the Associated Seminaries, even though the degree would be granted by the Associated Seminaries.

Let me begin by explaining why I have adopted the categories—professional and nonprofessional. I have adopted them for reasons of honesty, and because I believe that under certain circumstances, they can be defended within believers' church theology.

As for honesty, we must frankly acknowledge that we are in the business of turning out professional ministers. At least, we are expecting our graduates to perform duties under conditions that normally characterize the professions. Let me list at least six marks of the professions: (1) full or nearly fulltime employment; (2) full or nearly full support in the form of a salary; (3) special training (in the case of Protestant ministers this is normally a Bachelor of Divinity (BD) education); (4) special functions, i.e., functions or duties not expected of ordinary people; (5) membership in professional associations, guilds, unions, etc.; (6) consciousness of the existence of professional peers and professional standards set by peers.

It is evident that the Associated Mennonite Seminaries are dedicated in practice to the professional ministry, and that the Mennonite Church is moving toward the professional ministry. Indeed, certain branches of the church have had the professional ministry for many years. That this change could come about among the Old Mennonites, without critical examination, is, however, surprising. It is noteworthy that no church-wide conferences, no monographs, no crises have attended the decision of the church leaders to move in the direction of the professional ministry. This means that the transition has been considered either insignificant, or inevitable, or possibly, good in itself. It is assumed that by toning down the professional character of the professional ministry, and by making slight modifications, it is possible to adopt the professional ministry without undesirable results. For one thing, the language of the professional ministry is avoided. Hence, the editor of *The Mennonite Encyclopedia* struggles for a word and ends up with a substantive, such as, "single pastor with training and salary."[3] It is assumed that we can superimpose the Protestant patterns of the ministry on a brotherhood concept of the church by slight attitudinal and functional changes. In other words, a congregation may have a professional minister as if it had none if: (1) the minister were employed but not regulated as a typical employee; (2) he were paid, but not paid well; (3) he were trained, but trained in a Mennonite seminary; (4) he were expected to do professional duties while being called by his first name, i.e., avoiding the title, "Reverend"; (5) he were allowed to join ministerial associations without assuming leadership roles; (6) he were conscious of his professional peers, but not overly influenced by them. In other words, it is assumed that the Mennonites are either sufficiently clever or socially lethargic to adopt one system and reap the benefits of another. We can adopt a Protestant form of the ministry while having an Anabaptist, free church in reality. We can have a slightly modified Protestant form of ministry and an Anabaptist ecclesiology with its emphasis upon brotherhood, priesthood of all believers, and congregational initiative at the same time.

It is interesting to note that while *The Mennonite Encyclopedia* marks the transition from the so-called plural ministry to the "single pastor with training and full salary," it makes little of this transition, and the editor, with evident assurance of its rightness and inevitability, remarks with apparent surprise that "the practice of the single pastor with training and full or part salary has been slow in coming to the Mennonite Church (MC), but since World War II has been rapidly increasing, except in the four Eastern conferences—Franconia, Lancaster, Franklin-Washington, and Virginia, and in Western conferences of Iowa-Nebraska, North Central, and Pacific Coast." He notes that "Some sixty congregations, mostly in the Middle West, now have single pastors with salary."[4] The significance of the founding of the

3. Bender, "Ministry," 704.
4. Bender, "Ministry," 704.

Associated Mennonite Seminaries is not mentioned in the article on "The Ministry" in *The Mennonite Encyclopedia*, and the term "professional" is not used. This, it seems to me, is typical of the Mennonite desire to have a professional ministry without calling it such. The best interpretation we can put on this is that it is assumed that Mennonites can modify the single, salaried, trained ministry in such a way that the historic pitfalls of the Protestant pattern will be avoided. It is assumed that whereas the Protestant experience of the professional ministry has been at best ambiguous (Protestants having been unable to avoid professionalism and clericalism, etc.), Mennonites can avoid these wild fruits somehow. (It is ironical, to say the least, that just at that point in history that the Catholic Church and churches of the magisterial reformation discover the lay ministry, the Mennonites decide to give it up.) However, the unanswered question is: How can we avoid the pitfalls? How can we be sure that the professional ministry will not undermine such basic concepts as lay responsibility and initiative, brotherhood, and the priesthood and preacherhood of all believers? It seems to me that to answer this question is the peculiar responsibility of the seminaries, since they, presumably, know the issues, and are, indeed, in the practice of turning out—shall we call them—"single pastors with training and full salary," or shall we call them, "professional ministers"?

Possibly the professional ministry and the conception of the believers' church are not at odds, but if they are not, it is clear that the burden of proof lies not with our brethren on the bench but with those who decided to enter the business of turning out professional ministers. So far, I have seen no such proof, and I must confess that I cannot prove that the professional ministry can be contained within the believers' church concept. However, I would like to test a hypothesis—that the professional ministry is compatible with the believers' church if, and only if, the professional ministry is redefined within a total view of the ministry which stands in contrast to traditional Protestant presupposition and practice. In other words, it is possible to accept the professional ministry if our concept of the "ministry" is radically changed. Indeed, if we were to redefine the ministry as such, we may find that categories such as professional/nonprofessional are legitimate alternatives, and, indeed, are preferable to the categories of clergy and laity. For whereas we find it difficult to use the term, "clergy," because we don't believe in its sacramental, cultural, and legal connotations, and we find it awkward to use the term "laity" since we have rejected its logical counterpart, we can use the dichotomy of "professional" and "nonprofessional" as simple, non-theological, sociological terms standing for functional distinctions and functional distinctions only. The dichotomy of professional and nonprofessional is simply a way of stating the obvious.

What is the concept of the total ministry which would make the professional ministry a possibility within the believers' church tradition? It is a view according to which the ministry consists first and primarily of the work of nonprofessionals. By the nonprofessional ministry we mean men and women who are expected to fulfill all the traditional, biblical functions of the ministry including preaching, praying, prophesying, comforting, counseling, teaching, and administration. What this really implies is a plural ministry consisting of ordained men and women who may or may not be theologically trained, but, in any case, give part of their time and energies to the church. The important thing is that the nonprofessional ministry is considered to be primary and normative. It is "the ministry." Such a concept is a logical extension of the believers' church view of the charismatic structure of the church, of lay initiative, of brotherhood, and of the priesthood and preacherhood of all believers. What I am really arguing for is the "bench." I do not mean by that several handy laymen to help the preacher out now and then, or trustees, or members of a church council, or unordained elders who stand in the background. I am referring to a group of ministers, chosen because of their gifts, who assume active responsibility for the spiritual leadership and oversight of the congregation. Although they are nonprofessional, they are, nevertheless, ordained, and they are religious in the best sense of the word. Although we would do well to avoid any semblance of a religious or spiritual caste, professional or nonprofessional, these men would be chosen for their spiritual credentials: to the extent that they are spiritually qualified, the ministry would be accorded respect. These men would be chosen, not because they qualify by being technically trained, but because they are spiritually prepared to do the work of the ministry.

How, then, does the professional ministry fit in? The professional minister is properly seen as an aid to the nonprofessional ministers. The professional minister may be seen as a minister who offers technical knowledge and skills where these are lacking. He is intended to supply what the nonprofessionals do not ordinarily have, namely, adequate theological understanding and ecclesiological know-how. Furthermore, when a congregation reaches a certain size and complexity, it may need someone to serve full time as an overall supervisor of its pastoral functions. Hence, the professional minister.

The contribution, therefore, of the professional minister is mainly functional in character. He is not intended to make up for the spiritual inadequacy of the congregation. He is not called in order to bring spiritual strength, prophetic power, personal warmth, drive, or commitment to the congregation. The purpose of the professional minister is to coordinate, direct, advise, enable, and equip the various ministries of the church. It is precisely where spiritual gifts are rife that he is needed, particularly when the church's energies are likely to get out of hand without his direction. It should be pointed out that there is no place for the professional minister in a small congregation where the program is simple, unless the congregation is engaged in a specialized ministry requiring technical skill. For example, it may be necessary to have a specially trained minister for a congregation of twenty members in the inner city. At any rate, a professional minister should not be called to lead a small congregation under ordinary circumstances, even if it could afford one. The professional minister is called not for his spiritual gifts, though it may be hoped that he is gifted. The professional minister is not a spiritual bonanza. He is a "Christian technician" whose duty it is to "enable" the church to channel its energies toward constructive ends. I would not press the distinction between the nonprofessional minister and the professional minister so far as to insist that the one is religious and the other is less than religious, but I would say that what is distinctive about the nonprofessional minister is his spiritual gift, and what is distinctive about the professional minister is his technical knowledge.

The relation of the professional minister to the nonprofessional minister may be illustrated by the relation of the playing coach to the team. The coach is, to be sure, a player like the others. Hence, he will preach, teach, counsel, and pray along with the other ministers in the church. But he is hired, not primarily because of his playing ability, but because he knows the game and he is able to call the plays and enable others to play their positions well.[5] The seminary is a school for training playing coaches, and ministers are hired for their coaching ability.

---

5. The analogy of the playing coach is not perfect. It may seem to imply an authoritative role which would result in undermining the responsibilities of other ministers in policy-making. Let it be assumed that in practice the professional minister would lead through a process of group decision-making which, admittedly, a "playing coach" has neither the time nor possibly the disposition to negotiate. It should also be pointed out that the employment of more than one professional minister is a possibility.

The problem of the traditional Protestant conception of the professional ministry is that it expects the minister to take on the world and the devil alone while the congregation watches in the bleachers. Occasionally, one of the members would get out there and help him, but the professional is "the ministry." Not only does he play the game alone, but he is supposed to gather together within himself all of the graces and gifts of the church. He is, therefore, not only supposed to be the leader of the church, but also a religious man; indeed, he is prophet, priest, teacher, ruler, and ideal family man as well. The error of the Protestant concept lies not only in its exaggerated demands for technical and spiritual competence, but that it is a basically wrong understanding of the ministry. The ministry, properly speaking, belongs to all the people, of whom certain especially gifted ones may be ordained and to whom may be called a professional leader who will teach them what can be taught from books, and who will give them the kind of undivided service which fulltime employment makes possible.

Although I am not satisfied by the term, "pastoral director," as it is used by H. Richard Niebuhr in *The Purpose of the Church and Its Ministry*, I find it increasingly attractive.[6] To be sure, Niebuhr was informed by a certain sacramental and episcopal tradition, which we do not accept as our own, but I believe that the concept could be adapted to the believers' church tradition. According to this view, the professional minister would conceive of his job primarily in terms of "equipping" the congregation to function harmoniously and effectively. Niebuhr's view has often been criticized because it seems to emphasize the administrative side of the minister's duties to the neglect of the minister's role as preacher and prophet. This would be a valid criticism if it were assumed, as it frequently is in Protestantism, that the minister is an all-around athlete, but if it may be assumed that the prophetic functions of the church are distributed within the congregation, then the church is free to limit its demands to such expertise as a BD education can supply. It is, of course, good when a minister is gifted in all departments, but to demand it is ecclesiological heresy, and inhuman as well.

It may be argued that my view of the professional minister is "reductionist." I have shorn the minister of his spiritual splendor, mystery, and the religious uniqueness of his calling. My only defense is that the glory lies in the *ploroma*, i.e., the fullness, the abundance of gifts as they are distributed in the congregation. The professional also participates in the distribution of

---

6. Niebuhr, *Purpose*, chapter 2.

spiritual gifts, but he is hired, not for his spiritual gifts primarily, but for his technical knowledge and skills.

If this concept of the professional ministry seems to deprive the ministry of its religious aura, it does at least offer something which is needed by ministers today, namely, professional identity. A new source of identity is needed now because traditional identity-bestowing sources are disappearing. Catholic clergymen traditionally received their identity from sacramental and hierarchical sources, and Protestant clergymen received their identity from a sense of religious calling. But these are coming in for a drubbing by the concept of the church as the laity or the people. Priests and ministers are no longer so sure that they stand in a peculiar relation to God, and they are no longer so ready to assume the role of the "religious man" or the "religious professional." Indeed, they find that the only valid difference between them and the ordinary people of the church is functional in nature. They are prepared by educational advantage and by competence to do certain things that others cannot do, or do not have the opportunity to do. Therefore, what is needed to give the minister a proper sense of identity is his professional uniqueness. It seems to me that the minister deserves this, especially since he lives in a culture where identity is generally bestowed through one's profession. To accent the minister's professional uniqueness is simply to grant him what he has coming. A problem of a number of Mennonite ministers I know is that they find themselves in a professional limbo arising from the fact that the Mennonite Church, entirely too often, tries to solve the incongruity of an uncritically adopted Protestant pattern of the ministry in a believers' church context by depriving the minister of his professional identity. I would propose to the contrary that the Mennonite minister should be accepted as a professional alongside the doctors, lawyers, bankers, scholars, and farmers. His professional status should be seen as that which is bestowed upon him on the same basis as any other profession. The way to guard against professionalism is not to deny him his professional identity, but to distinguish between what is intrinsically religious and what is intrinsically professional.

Now we will turn to the model for the training of the professional ministry. Training for the professional ministry would begin on Level III; i.e., the third year. Previous to this, the student would have had two years of theological education designed primarily to meet the needs of the nonprofessional minister. He learns how to be a nonprofessional before he learns to be a professional. By the end of the second year, he would have a reasonable understanding of Christian theology, and he would have grasped the concept of the believers' church, especially with respect to discipleship and church life and order.

With this background, he would enroll for his third year at a school other than his denominational seminary. His education from this point on would be ecumenical. His choice would depend upon the kind of ministry he envisages. If his plans were to be the pastor of a typical congregation, he would enroll at a school where the so-called "parish ministry" is still believed in and emphasized (Yale); if he were interested in the urban ministry, he would choose a year at a school such as the University of Chicago which has access to the urban training center; if he were interested in counseling, he would choose a school such as Southern Baptist Theological Seminary; and if he were interested in teaching, he might consider a doctoral program at an American or European university setting.

In some cases, students would wish to take a third and a fourth year, thus combining an academic year with an internship, or a year of voluntary service. Flexibility would be essential in order to match the student's needs with appropriate resources. It should be pointed out that one of the working committees of the American Association of Theological Schools, in the current study of future needs of theological education, is proposing the establishment of a number of training centers in connection with an elaborate scheme for the consolidation of theological resources of the nation. Such centers could be designed to offer specialized pastoral training. It is conceivable that many or most small denominational seminaries could enter into an overall ecumenical plan of cooperation for the establishment of such centers, thus reducing their curriculum to two years.

Integral to the concept of Level III education for the professional ministry is the concept of the professional ministry as a specialized ministry. All professional ministries should be considered specialized. Even men who are trained for the "parish ministry" should be trained as specialists. Their specialization is the "parish ministry," while others specialize in the urban ministry, hospital chaplaincy, college chaplaincy, etc. It may be argued that by regarding the parish ministry as a specialized ministry one of the most evident sources of unrest among ministers would be removed. Instead of feeling, as many do, that they are general jacks-of-all-trades because they are not inner-city specialists or chaplains, they could feel that they have a distinctive ministry which is a specialization in itself.

There are at least three reasons why I propose that the third year should be taken at a location other than at the denominational seminary. In the first place, it would provide the student with an ecumenical experience appropriate to an ecumenical age. That ecumenical experience is a good thing need not be argued at length. Ecumenical experience is broadening, liberating, and exhilarating. That advantage, which is accepted as normal for the faculty by virtue of their having received the doctorate at a non-Mennonite school, should become the privilege of students as well. Indeed, it is needed in order to provide perspective by which students may examine critically their own denominational heritage. Ecumenical experience provides students an opportunity to encounter firsthand outstanding authorities within their own specialty, and the opportunity to engage fellow students of other traditions in conversation is training for ecumenical cooperation on the level of the local church. Putting it negatively, a student who has been brought up in a Mennonite community, educated at a Mennonite college, trained in a Mennonite seminary, and returned to a Mennonite church is not likely to be fully prepared to meet other churches and the world. Educational incest is a problem facing many small denominational seminaries. No measure of excellence on the part of denominational education can compensate for the lack of ecumenical experience.

Ecumenicity, however, is a two-way street. Accordingly, it is proposed that denominational schools like the Associated Mennonite Seminaries should be encouraged to contribute to the larger theological enterprise by attracting students from other denominational schools who are interested in the tradition. Students in the larger interdenominational schools could spend a semester or a year of their BD program at a place like the Associated Mennonite Seminaries. Here they would encounter the Anabaptist-believers' church point of view, and, of course, it would challenge the Associated Mennonite Seminaries to rethink their message to the world in order to put it into terms which command contemporary attention. Thus, it is conceivable that a great deal of ecumenical sharing would be the result.

A second reason why it is advisable for students to take their third year elsewhere is that they would be able to choose a seminary or university where their special interests could be met at the highest level of competence. It is obvious that the small, denominational seminary simply cannot offer the full range of courses and clinical facilities needed for every specialization. In a period of increasing specialization, it can no longer be expected that all seminaries can do everything that needs to be done. In the future, I am quite certain that seminaries generally will justify their existence by emphasizing particular areas of knowledge or training upon agreement with other institutions. Another reason why a third year under ecumenical circumstances may be appropriate is that it would enable small schools to conserve and concentrate their energies. By offering only two years, the cost in faculty and sources would be reduced, and it would enable the small seminaries to do what they can do exceedingly well without their trying to do everything.

Nonprofessional Theological Education

The concept of Nonprofessional Theological Education which I am about to propose is a radical one. Let me say in advance that I am conscious of its problematic character, but I trust that it is at least worthy of consideration. Its justification, if it can be justified at all, lies in the fact that it proceeds directly from the concept of the believers' church, and it is an attempt to come to terms with the mood of youth today. It is intended to carry some of the implications of the believers' church into the form of theological education as well as the purpose of theological education.

As to the form of theological education, it would attempt to make theological education in itself an experience of the believers' church. This rests on the assumption that education for the believers' church and experience of the church cannot be separated. It is an attempt to answer the question about what it means for a seminary to prepare men and women for the ministry in a church which emphasizes the ministry of the laity, brotherhood, discipline, discipleship, and confessional and structural flexibility. As for the purpose of theological education, my proposal looks toward broadening the scope of theological education and, indeed, a drastic refocusing thereof. If it were successful, it would change the character of the whole enterprise. I am tempted to say it would revolutionize theological education.

What should be the primary purpose of theological education in the believers' church tradition? It should be the training of the laity, or I would prefer the term, "nonprofessionals." I would like to see the Associated Mennonite Seminaries become the first institution of its kind to carry out the implications of the theology of the laity into the field of theological education. Insofar as other traditions are accepting in principle the concept of the ministry of the laity, this proposal would have broad implications.

It is my feeling that the renaissance of the laity has been largely ineffectual, because it has left the structure of the ministry unchallenged. It has made certain claims about the fact that the church consists of the laity, but the end result is little more than to work the people into a frenzy of activities, many of which are meaningless, while the ministry has remained essentially unchanged. The term, "lay ministry," has been used largely to mean what laymen do and always have done, only more so, while ministers do what they have done no less.

The possibility that the ministry of the laity means that nonprofessionals may assume those traditional responsibilities once reserved for the clergy is seldom seriously considered by the most vocal advocates of the laity. Hence the renaissance of the laity is after all a relatively conservative movement. It leaves the structure of the ministry unchanged. Furthermore, by virtue of the fact that the renaissance of the laity has not challenged clerical structures as such, theological education has not been forced to respond, except theologically. My own view, however, is that insofar as theologians are responsible to work out the practical implications of their insights, they ought to lead the church into patterns which would incorporate these insights. I would, therefore, propose that an institution such as the Associated Mennonite Seminaries would do well to lead in the restructuring of the ministry by offering a program in anticipation of basic structural change.

I am proposing a concept of the ministry which is first and foremost nonprofessional. It is a concept of the plural ministry, in which a number of brethren would be chosen to lead the congregation according to their gifts. The ministry would be charismatic in principle. It follows, however, that in many instances, gifts need to be informed and trained. Therefore, a way must be found by which the charismatic principle and theological education can be joined. This to my knowledge has not been done. In place of the charismatic principle, we have substituted a degree program which becomes in itself the prerequisite to ordination. The discernment of gifts is a minor part of theological education simply by virtue of the fact that it is organized as a school and students are examined almost exclusively on the basis of their academic ability. It is just a bit ludicrous for seminaries in the free church tradition to uphold and adulate the New Testament charismatic structure of the congregation from within a system which either denies it in practice or limits it to the selection of Sunday school teachers. What we must do, therefore, is to structure theological education in such a way that the discernment of gifts is part of the educational process. This would mean that the reality of the church would be brought into the life of the seminary. This, I believe, can be done without sacrificing the integrity of the seminary as an educational institution. In other words, the seminary would be organized not only to impart knowledge and to improve skills, but to help students to understand themselves in relation to the purposes of God in the church and in the world.

Before going into detail about the kind of ministry that is envisaged and the general atmosphere of the seminary so conceived, let me set forth the broad outline of the model.

Seminary education would begin with Level II. The purpose of Level II would be threefold. It would be intended: (1) to prepare men for commissioning as ministers and missionaries; (2) to grant a two-year degree (Master of Theological Studies); and (3) to provide the first two years of a BD program. What do we mean by commissioning? We mean authorization by the church, upon the joint recommendation by the seminary and a congregation (home congregation) to "preach and baptize." Commissioning would correspond to the Anabaptist practice of "sending." It would be a general mandate to do the work of an "apostle," or a minister, looking in most instances to the establishment of a new congregation. It is assumed that the minister would be nonprofessional insofar as he would practice a secular profession, and his ministry would be pursued alongside his profession.

The length of time from admission to commissioning would vary from person to person depending upon his previous experience, his understanding, and his development. The intention would be to commission him as soon as possible. It would most certainly require one year and possibly one and a half or two years. The decision of when to commission a student would be made jointly by a seminary panel consisting of faculty and students, together with a congregation—presumably his home congregation. That commissioning would not depend upon the completion of a set number of courses; indeed, the fact that commissioning may not occur at all would add a dramatic quality to the educational process. The educational process would also presuppose a kind of intersubjectivity which does not always occur even in small denominational seminaries. Students who desire a nonprofessional degree along with or without commissioning would be given a MTS degree (note, this is not an MA) after completion of two years.

In some cases, hopefully in many cases, students would decide to make the ministry a profession as well as a religious calling. In such an event, students would enter Level III for a year or more at another school, leading to the BD or possibly to a more advanced professional or academic degree.

What forms would the nonprofessional ministry take? It could take at least three forms: (1) missionary witness leading to the establishment of congregations; (2) ministry in established congregations; (3) ministry in secular contexts outside the congregation. Sometimes several of these could be combined.

The first of these would involve the commission to bring new congregations into existence as opportunity would arise in connection with a secular occupation. Assuming that Mennonite young people will increasingly locate in urban centers where there are by no means an abundance of Mennonite churches, the missioner would attempt to bring a congregation into existence as his real calling. Although it would be presumptuous to suggest a single technique, he would very likely begin by organizing a fellowship for discussion and study. Participants would probably consist of a few fellow Christians, possibly a few fellow Mennonites, if there are some around, and non-Christians with whom he has become acquainted in connection with his profession or in the neighborhood. The fellowship may continue, or it may dwindle, but if the interest of the participants were to continue, the question of the organization of the fellowship into a church would become the next step. Then the question would arise as to what it would mean to be a church. That is to say, the whole question of the nature and the mission of the church would come to the fore. At this point, the Mennonite conception of the church as a brotherhood under nonprofessional leadership would become relevant, and the intrinsic freedom of Mennonite ecclesiology to adapt to new social situations and to improvise could guide the developing organization, whether it was understood to be Mennonite or not. The fact that the church is defined as a fellowship of believers instead of a building or a hierarchy is an important point in itself. Hopefully, in many cases a congregation (house church) would result, in which case it may decide to become a Mennonite church, though that would not be the most important issue.

With the reorganization of theological education toward the nonprofessional ministry, new ways would have to be found by which nonprofessionals could actually bring churches to birth. Commissioning would involve a life commitment to extend the rule of Christ through the extension of the church, and the latest and most radical techniques of evangelism and church extension would be employed. The appeal to the younger generation to enter the seminary would be the opportunity to bring new kinds of churches into being, using new techniques which depended upon improvisation. The appeal would be for the younger generation to give concrete expression to the church and churchmanship anew under the guidance of the Holy Spirit. Freedom to experiment would, hopefully, attract the rebels who have broken with traditional patterns of church life.

A program of nonprofessional theological education would also seek to prepare young men and women to serve in established congregations. Their contributions would, of course, depend on their gifts and the needs of the various congregations. In some cases, they would be ordained to the plural ministry along with or without the professional minister. In other cases, they would assist as pillars in the congregation or as youth leaders.

A third kind of nonprofessional minister would seek to witness in the secular structure with a more than incidental Christian thrust. He would seek to understand how Christ can be brought to bear upon secular institutions and structures in which he is involved. He would not necessarily seek to create new congregations, but he would bring the grace and judgment of Christ to bear upon the areas of life in which he is involved. Whether his witness would have to do with questions of values or of justice, it would be done with Christian motivation and with a kind of perspicuity which a year or more of theology had made possible.

Those who attempt to witness in secular structures would benefit by the experience of Metropolitan Associates, a group of people in Philadelphia who have taken secular jobs in municipal government offices and in industry in order to test the possibilities of witness and develop techniques. An entire curriculum of questions and procedures is being developed in order to help lay people to understand what is going on in secular structures and know how to influence secular structures.

The curriculum would resemble in many respects a standard BD curriculum. However, teaching methods would vary considerably. Although the lecture method would be used, seminars and independent reading and the tutorial system would tend to predominate. Exchange of ideas would be encouraged, and subjects would be discussed on an existential level. The subject matter would become increasingly lay in the sense that theology would be approached not only or primarily from the standpoint of traditional disciplines, but from the standpoint of problems of modern man. To be sure, there are materials that need to be learned for their kerygmatic value, but they would not include as much historical background as is often considered necessary by the theologians. A course in James, which actually got to chapter 1, verse 15, by the end of the term, is an extreme case of the kind of academic imperialism that would not be tolerated. James would be studied primarily for its message and its function in the community.

A seminary for the training of lay ministers would not lower its standards, but it would not attempt to give a completely well-rounded theological education—whatever that is. It would seek to prepare men to live and to witness for Christ—not to produce academicians. This means that the starting point would be living problems facing modern man and the church as it seeks to be faithful and as it seeks to serve the world. Furthermore, the seminary would not attempt to encapsulate all of truth in a system which has to be mastered whether it is relevant or not. The free church non-creedal approach to doctrine would mean the seminary is free to find answers wherever they can be found without necessarily developing its own systems. The attempt to train nonprofessionals would mean the development of lay theology which would be no less profound in content than traditional theology, but it would tend to be less technical and more human and relevant.

Now concerning the general atmosphere of the seminary. Although the seminary would remain a seminary and would not claim to be a church, nevertheless, some of the functions of the believers' church would be structured in the seminary. Students and faculty would become a spiritual fellowship. Whereas the center of the religious life in most Protestant seminaries is daily chapel, the center of fellowship in my model would be a disciplined study seminar, which would be under the leadership of the students and to which would be attached a faculty member. This seminar would be home base for each student. This seminar would assume responsibility to see that its members meet the qualifications for commissioning. This means ultimate responsibility for the spiritual, emotional, and academic development of the student. The seminar would help the student to know himself in relation to Christ and the needs of the church and the world. In this context, students would wrestle with their problems of alienation, vocation, and a Christian style of life. Experience in the seminar would be centered on existence clarification, involving intense personal encounter and intersubjectivity.

Since it may be assumed that Level II would attract many students whose faith is unsettled, and whose understanding of themselves and the world is unclear, demands would be laid upon the faculty to go beyond technical competence in their field. They would have to articulate the faith in a way that would make sense to the younger generation. Assuming that many of the answers which once satisfied the faculty no longer satisfy the contemporary student, the faculty would have to listen to the students and increasingly shape their theology around student (lay) problems. Entirely too much theology today is an attempt to answer questions which are no longer asked. Indeed, one of the implications of nonprofessional education is that it would strive for authenticity by being no longer tempted to encapsulate truth in trite professional formulas. It would be assumed that students without professional ambitions would make their ministry dependent upon the ability of the school to make Christianity meaningful and to motivate them to make the ministry their true calling in life.

This may be the time to discuss the mentality of the student who could be expected to be attracted by such a curriculum. It would attract the questing student who is looking for a faith to which he can commit himself—a faith to which he can commit himself wholeheartedly, because it makes sense. It would appeal initially to students of whom many would not be in a position to commit themselves to the professional ministry because they are not convinced of the relevance of Christianity or because the church as they have experienced it appears unattractive. We should note that the fact that many students today are unable to commit themselves in advance to the church cannot be attributed to personal inadequacies but simply to the culture in which they have been brought up. Therefore, it would behoove us to accept as a legitimate and, indeed, as a creative response, the setting up of a theological program designed for our cultural offspring as they are. Even regular denominational schools are finding that a high percentage of incoming students are not committed to the ministry. Rather, students are looking for a framework of meaning, a basis for morality, and an interpretation of contemporary history. Their skepticism of traditional Christian formulations is, however, off-set by an almost naive openness to new possibilities.

One important aspect of group experience would be discernment of gifts. Students would help each other to decide what they have to bring to the ministry, and this would be especially important since, having broken with the Protestant concept of the ministry, it is considered normal that individuals are not gifted in all departments. Such an experience of spiritual discernment would mean that the seminary is to that extent engaged in one of the essential practices of the believers' church.

You will notice that the model which I am proposing includes college preparation. Although specific college courses would not be prerequisite for admission to Level II, I would propose a way of telescoping college preparation and seminary education so that students would enter the seminary with nearly a half year of theology under the belt. I would propose that college students who are interested in seminary work—indeed, I would recommend that students generally—should be encouraged to postpone their study of college Bible or religion until the junior and senior years, preferably the latter. They would then take courses on a level comparable to seminary, and I would go so far as to suggest that the Associated Mennonite Seminaries would seek a cooperative arrangement with certain Mennonite colleges which would enable seminary professors to be loaned for periods of time to the colleges in order to teach senior courses corresponding roughly to introductory courses in seminaries. Therefore, students would be able to come to seminary with ten to fifteen hours of theology. I realize that the accrediting agencies would look with horror upon such an arrangement, but if this were seen as part of a new conception of theological education, it would conceivably merit separate consideration.

Obviously adjustments would have to be made in the college curriculum, but I am personally of the opinion that if students were to wait until their senior year for high-level courses in religion, they would be ahead. Lower-level Bible too often consists of baby courses which are intended to make up for poor Sunday schools, and to facilitate the adjustment from a conservative to a critical approach to the Bible. It is my view that if students were to get their philosophy and classics before studying Genesis, the struggle would be lifted to an altogether different level. Students who know Greek mythology have no trouble accepting Hebrew mythology. Religion would then be regarded not as an adjustment to or protection from secular knowledge, but as a means to come to terms with reality.

I am also proposing supervised summer internships following college as an integral part of the program. Internships would vary in kind, but many students would profit most by experience in cities in cooperation with such centers as the Urban Training Center in Chicago and M.U.S.T. in New York City. This would be the occasion for the students to encounter the world which they would learn to love in order to serve, and it would fill them with questions which it would be the business of the seminary to answer during their further preparation.

One of the questions which must be going through your heads is the question of the practicality of nonprofessional theological education. Would it be possible to interest a sufficiently large number of people to make it a possibility? It could be argued that there is currently a strong reaction against the church among young people; that secularization and affluence fail to provide the religious atmosphere that would be necessary to get it off the ground. Furthermore, it could be argued that students who insist upon early marriage and graduate school in one of the secular sciences would not be willing to take a year or more out just to get ready for a religious avocation. Once more it could be argued that the whole concept of the nonprofessional ministry is impractical due to the conflict between professional demands and ministerial duties. So-called lay people just don't have the time.

I find it difficult to answer these objections. Only those who are intimately acquainted with current Mennonite attitudes in relation to the larger cultural ethos are competent at this point. I believe, however, that the program could be made to appeal to many of our young people if the program took their mentality seriously. One thing is certain: we cannot attract them on the same basis that my generation was attracted. I doubt whether young people will be moved by appeal to authority and to history as some of us were. Neither the entire Bible nor the church can be made to appeal on the basis of authority. Furthermore, I doubt whether the Anabaptist Vision can be expected to move the present generation with power comparable to the power with which it moved my generation of young churchmen and scholars. And talk about the establishment of the true church, which has been so much a part of our heritage, is now under judgment for its simplistic naivete.

However, I believe that the present generation of young people will respond to new formulations of the Christian hope for the church and for the world if these can meet the tests of reality. What the younger generation will not tolerate is phoniness or at least what appears to them as phoniness. Somehow the suspicion that the church is less than candid, that the church conceals its own uncertainties and doubts, that the church refuses to acknowledge its failures, and that the church not infrequently falls ethically below the best in humanism must be taken seriously. The proposal which I am making would attempt to meet this kind of criticism by inviting young people, even those who are critical of the church and uncertain of their commitment, to join the search for authentic faith, obedience, and faithful forms of church life.

I have no idea how many students would respond to such a program as I have outlined, but if we were to assume that those who would come to the Associated Mennonite Seminaries under its present system would come anyhow (and I believe that they would) the total number would rise rather than diminish. It is conceivable that once the program gets underway, the total enrollment could increase from 25 to 50 percent.

One other aspect of the total proposal should be mentioned at this time. It would be to look directly to the churches for enrollment by showing them how to go about enlisting ministers from their ranks. Indeed, quite apart from enrollment prospects, this would be a logical task within the general framework of the redefinition of the ministry. Congregations would be encouraged and shown how to discover potential ministerial leadership among them, and, in some cases, such potential ministers would be encouraged to spend a year or more at the Associated Mennonite Seminaries at the church's expense. Undoubtedly, this has already happened in certain cases, but it would be much more likely to happen if theological education were designed for the nonprofessional. It is no longer a question of potential qualifications of farmers but of college graduates, sometimes with advanced degrees, who have the brains, and frequently the interest, to become ministers, but have no conception of the role of the nonprofessional minister. I would express the hope that before all traces of the historic conception of the plural nonprofessional ministry disappear from our consciousness, or before we come to the erroneous conclusion that the plural ministry should be associated with conservative, unenlightened past, we would do well to explore it as the method of the future.

10

Marginalia (excerpt, 1969)

Virgil Vogt

I am extremely grateful for the articles which appear in this issue of *Concern*, for they focus attention on one of the major hindrances in any move toward the renewal of the church. Ministers, in my acquaintance, are much more a part of the problem than most of they realize. By accepting so many important churchly functions and dimensions of his own role, the average minister severely limits any possibility of a spiritual breakthrough while he, at the same time, knocks himself out trying to engineer one.

The ministerial stereotype has become so widespread in our culture that it is extremely difficult for any one of us to get beyond it to consider meaningful new alternatives. Too many "new" concepts of ministry are simply variations on the same old theme. As an illustration of how subtle and pervasive this stereotype is, I would suggest that I see it creeping back into J. Lawrence Burkholder's proposals while he is in the process of trying to throw it out.

The main lines of Burkholder's argument do, of course, challenge this ministerial stereotype at a foundational level. I find his statement of the issues refreshing and significant. His intention is clear—he wants the plural, non-professional ministry to become "the ministry." But when he begins spelling out how a professional minister relates to the professional, plural ministry, some of the old assumptions get back in.

For instance, why should it be assumed that the professional minister will be the playing coach? Is it not equally conceivable that one of the non-professional ministers will have the gift of knowing what to do next, or will know so much more about the local situation, so as to be most qualified to function in this role? The chief defect in this illustration is not, as Burkholder suggests in his footnote, in what it may imply about the way decisions are made, but in the assumption that the professional is still the one who leads the others. The role of the technical expert is not necessarily to know what needs to be done, but to be good at doing certain difficult jobs well.

Elsewhere the same problem creeps into Burkholder's discussion. He still envisions the professional as the "over-all supervisor" or the one who "directs." In corporate management the well-trained specialist is not necessarily the best over-all director. These are different functions. This is even more true within the church. The simple assumption that seminary trained specialists are best qualified as "congregational supervisors" is at the heart of a great deal of our confusion.

Some of the old assumptions are probably operating when Burkholder suggests that "the parish ministry" could be one of the specializations for professional training. The whole point of his article is that there is no such thing as "the" parish ministry; there are many parish ministries. Specialization would therefore involve developing capabilities in one or several of these many kinds of parish ministry. Thus a serious application of Burkholder's insights might lead some young professional to prepare for teaching in the local congregation, or for personal counseling in the local congregation, or for social action in the local congregation, or administration in the local congregation, or evangelism in the local congregation, or music leadership in the local congregation. Persons who had thus focused their study and developed their abilities could be extremely useful in the church. But specialists in "the parish ministry" is what BD programs have been about all along.

These are not meant as serious criticisms of the Burkholder paper. As a whole, he carries forward his stated task with consistency and creative vigor. They are simply meant to illustrate how easy it is for the old assumptions to get back into our thinking. This should no doubt alert us to the difficulty we will experience in any local congregation which makes a serious attempt at utilizing this kind of plural ministry Although the pitfalls are many, the potential advantages of a shared ministry are so overwhelming that I hope the risk is undertaken in many places in the immediate future.

It should also be noted here that the Burkholder and Klaassen articles presuppose a "Mennonite" audience in a way that no longer fits *Concern*, or the times in which we live. However, this does not reflect the authors' parochialism, but grows from the fact that both were addressing Mennonite audiences when they drafted their papers. Even though most writers and most readers of *Concern* are Mennonites, it no longer seems right to carry on the discussion about church renewal as though either the questions or the answers are uniquely denominational. Even so, a "word" addressed to a particular denomination may have considerable meaning and relevance to persons in other denominations and settings. It is with this confidence that we have retained the specificity of the original Burkholder and Klaassen materials.

Part II

On Communal Authority, "Order," and Discipline

11

Studies in Church Discipline

A Review Article

Elmer Ediger

Shelly, Maynard, ed. *Studies in Church Discipline*:
Newton: Mennonite Publication Office, 1958.[1]

This attractive paperback is important not only for its contents but for the step it represents in a process. One must see it in the perspective of a "concerned" type of stirring in General Conference Mennonite Church (GCMC) congregations toward a more vital church life. In this sense the method by which this book came to be and how it is to be used are in themselves implementation of a disciplinary process in keeping with a brotherhood concept of the church.

The more immediate context for this source book "designed to promote study and discussion on the local level" are the study conferences which were set in motion with the inter-Mennonite Winona Peace Study Conference in 1950 and for the General Conference Mennonites more particularly the Eden Peace Study Conference held in 1953. Although the Eden Conference was focused on the study of nonresistance it was within the larger context of the church and the gospel.

At the Eden Conference, Peter J. Dyck presented a paper on "The General Conference Approach to the Believers' Church." In this paper he observed that "The General Conference is suffering because of lack of a

---

1. This study was authorized by the General Conference Mennonite Church (GCMC) and prepared by its Discipline Study Committee.

clear concept of the church." In his final paragraph he says, "I see no reason why the predicted sect-cycle must complete its course. We can prevent a complete return and accommodation to society; we do not need to throw in our lot with watered-down Protestantism."[2]

In the ensuing discussion one group led by E. G. Kaufman made a proposal later adopted by the entire Peace Study Conference. It was suggested that the General Conference sponsor a study conference on the concept of the church, to wrestle with questions such as the following: "Is our present General Conference Church still true to the Anabaptist concept of a fellowship of the redeemed, living in common discipleship to the Lord Jesus Christ? . . . In keeping with our concept of the church, how do we revive those aspects of our faith which have been all but lost?"[3]

As a result, two years later the General Conference sponsored a study conference on "The Believers' Church" and subsequently published a significant report.[4] It was this conference which recommended that a special committee study the question of church discipline and which recommendation led to this book.

One of the most intense discussions of the Believers' Church Conference was with regard to church discipline. Although it was quite obvious that many of those present were steeled against any re-innovation of a church discipline comparable to that they remembered from their earlier church life, the searching and "talking-up" process (as Littell describes the brotherhood-sharing among believers) did bring about an amazing degree of fellowship and general agreement in regard to the importance of a redemptive discipline. "We recognize that the practice of Scriptural discipline is a necessary characteristic of a believers' church. We confess that our traditional patterns of discipline have often been negative, legalistic, harsh, and unloving, and hence, have not always contributed to the repentance and restoration of the fallen one. Moreover, we confess that we have often failed to deal effectively with the sins of the spirit and the sins of human relationships which are often difficult to identify."[5]

> We affirm that Scriptural discipline must be constructive and corrective in approach, redemptive in spirit, and must seek to employ all the varied ministries of the church. Such discipline finds birth

2. Dyck, "General Conference," D70, D76.
3. GCMC, "Toward a Revived," E20.
4. GCMC, *Proceedings*.
5. GCMC, *Proceedings*, 223.

within the brotherhood through prayer and Bible study, fellowship, and a process of mutual sharing resulting in corporate agreement as to the standards which are to be maintained. It seeks to reclaim the offender, to attain purity and order in the church, and to recall the whole brotherhood to the life of discipleship in Jesus Christ. It operates, therefore, in a setting of suffering love, a thorough teaching and counseling ministry, and a repentant brotherhood.[6]

Although it was not clear just how they would work and how the non-legislative General Conference would be involved, a Discipline Study Committee was appointed as part of the work of the Board of Education and Publication. Members of the committee, all contributors to this book, included Jacob T. Friesen, chairman, Cornelius J. Dyck, Henry Poettcker, A. E. Kreider, and Maynard Shelly. The committee rather deliberately ruled out any immediate goal of a definitive statement to be presented to the General Conference. This they felt would have ignored the principle "that the local fellowship of believers is the primary group in which God makes known His will under the direction of His Holy Spirit."[7] It also ruled out the possibility of another study conference.

The more creative approach, resulting in a source book and many local study groups, evolved when the committee began thinking of themselves as a searching fellowship. Members were given assignments on various aspects and presented papers to each other. At the same time that this official committee searching was going on, sometimes in week-long sessions, some other aftereffects of the Chicago Believers' Church Conference were simmering in the Western District. Here "Inter-Congregational Deputations" were carrying discipline concerns to individual congregational discussion.[8]

Representatives of different congregations in team fashion had prepared presentations on such subjects as divorce and remarriage, race prejudice, business ethics, lodges, liquor, leisure, and Sunday work. These papers prepared for congregations were also presented to the Discipline Study Committee and some were included in this book.

The committee then accepted the following goal and procedure: "The development of a thorough biblical and historical study; the preparation of a source book to promote the study of church discipline by individuals and groups; the sharing of findings of study groups from which the

---

6. GCMC, *Proceedings*, 223.
7. Friesen and Shelly, "Introduction," x.
8. GCMC, *Proceedings*, 11.

Discipline Study Committee would draw together a statement of findings and prepare a report to the next session of General Conference, indicating the direction the Holy Spirit is leading our brotherhood; and the incorporation into later editions of this book the findings of local and conference studies that these may become a further guide and inspiration to an ongoing study, leading to a deepening of the spiritual life of our fellowship and a renewal of life in Christ."[9]

The table of contents divides the book into three main categories. Under "Vision," covering the first hundred pages are the following nine articles:

> "The Disciplined Life" by J. N. Smucker
> "Love Working Through People" by Cornelius J. Dyck
> "The New Testament Community" by Henry Poettcker
> "Early Ideas of Authority" by Cornelius J. Dyck
> "Brotherly Discipline by the Early Swiss" by Robert Kreider
> "Menno and Discipleship" by Cornelius Krahn
> "Transformed in Nonconformity" by Harold W. Buller
> "Personality and Discipline" by Marvin Ewert
> "Standards with Love" by A. E. Kreider

The second section dealing with "Practice" covers another hundred pages and nine articles.

> "Where Do We Begin?" by Jacob T. Friesen
> "Marriage and Divorce" by Henry Poettcker
> "Healing Racial Divisions" by Esko W. Loewen
> "Right Conduct for Ministers" by Henry A. Fast
> "Business Ethics and Scriptural Teaching" by Jacob W. Nickel
> "Loyalty and Lodges" by David Schroeder and Esko W. Loewen
> "Life Without Liquor" by Albert M. Gaeddert
> "Leisure's New Meaning" by O'Ray C. Graber
> "A Spiritual Day of Rest" by L. R. Amstutz

The third section of "Reference Materials" includes a unique study article presumably by the editor presenting fourteen "hard problems" representing real situations for a case discussion approach in the local congregation. The appendix includes "Church Discipline Practices," a report of a survey made by Maynard Shelly for the Believers' Church Conference to study what is actually happening with regard to some of the measurable aspects of congregational discipline.

9. Friesen and Shelly, "Introduction," xi.

Also in the appendix are guiding principles for ministers and churches with regard to the minister-and-congregation relationships, a statement on the Believers' Church, "A Christian Declaration on Peace, War, and Military Service" and "Arguments Advanced Against Secret Societies" as prepared by A. D. Wenger in a Scottdale-published leaflet. The bibliography, the general index, and index of Scripture have been done very thoroughly and should be a very usable section of the book for local congregations and for other individual studies in this field.

Composed of contributions from nineteen individuals in the two major sections, there is remarkably little overlapping, but they are definitely individual contributions. This in a sense represents a "talking-up" of individuals in a somewhat congregational fashion with some consensus clearly evident. The writers, who are largely ministers and church schoolteachers, were apparently not chosen, however, to get a balanced representation of General Conference thinking. The weight is definitely on the side of those who are "concerned" with the restoration of a clearer sense of the church, particularly a brotherhood church. With the exception of Marvin Ewert, who has made a special study in the field of religion and personality, there has not been a tapping of those who have specialized outside of the biblical, historical and theological fields. Future contributions in the fields of business ethics and leisure could also include more of the concerned laity.

To give somewhat of a cross-sectional view of thinking on the approach to church discipline, we present here some key statements from writers, particularly from the first section of the book.

J. N. Smucker in writing about "The Disciplined Life" says,

> A life that is not properly disciplined is decadent, and our lack of inner controls is responsible for much of our tensions and the havocs caused thereby.... Strange that we understand and assent to the principle of discipline in the natural world but attempt to disregard it in the spiritual world.... To achieve a well-ordered and disciplined life we must begin at the center and not at the circumference. It is hopeless to try to shape a good life by merely putting up a list of rules and trying to force ourselves to follow them.... Church discipline is a baffling problem. But does not the real answer lie in the spiritual discipline of the self?[10]

C. J. Dyck on "Love Working Through People" presents the redemptive church community as a prerequisite for redemptive discipline:

---

10. Smucker, "Disciplined Life," 3, 4, 6.

PART II: ON COMMUNAL AUTHORITY, "ORDER," AND DISCIPLINE

> The climate of this community of love is safe enough to permit mistakes. You stumble and fall because I have not had time for you, or understanding, or love. Therefore, your sin is also my sin and in our solidarity of guilt we are not judged by the other but by our God, who is merciful through Jesus Christ. Because He takes us as we are, we learn to take each other as we are; and if improvements must be made, we begin from there.[11]

Henry Poettcker, though sensitive to the individual dynamic which C. J. Dyck underscores, points to the Old and New Testament discipline to learn

> how God went about educating His people for the task and the purpose which He had for them. Here was a covenant-relationship, which for our purposes we may see as a teacher-pupil relationship, to understand how God instructed and Israel learned. But more than that, this was a love-relationship, something that makes the dealings of God with man much more meaningful, and without which God's actions actually cannot be understood.
>
> "But this relationship was broken again and again.... God was not willing just to forget about Israel.... He chose to discipline."[12]

Poettcker devotes considerable time to word study, to rescue the word "discipline" from misconceptions or partial definitions and thus to see again the positive note. In closing Poettcker says, "We would reemphasize that, in order to practice church discipline, we need to see the new life of Christ, we need to see the true essence of the fellowship and we need to see the dominant role of the Holy Spirit."[13]

Cornelius J. Dyck on "Early Ideas of Authority" says in his introduction that

> the fact that most Mennonite schisms have been over matters of discipline indicates that real consensus about authority was, after all, only infrequently achieved in spite of explicit adherence to the *sola Scriptura* principle of the Reformation. Thus, the Mennonite Church has frequently failed to recognize one of its primary problems as that of authority, of the relationship of the Scriptures to the tradition and the normative function of both. Also, the doctrine of the Holy Spirit has actually tended to embarrass our pulpits....[14]

11. Dyck, "Love Working," 10.
12. Poettcker, "New Testament," 14.
13. Poettcker, "New Testament," 33–34.
14. Dyck, "Early Ideas," 35–36.

> Standing out in bold relief in this early picture is a very contemporary problem: tendency for the creative life of the Spirit to routinize and become rigid with the passing generations. Involved here is the loss of the brotherhood principle and the growth of the clerical order. But when the brotherhood disappears, discipline tends to become impersonal and thereby ineffective. It becomes punitive, not redemptive; mechanical, not spiritual. . . . By the very nature of the problem no solution can conceivably be found except "for our time." And even when we believe to have found adequate doctrine and method we dare never rest, lest violence be done to individual need of the brother. To codify discipline is to revert to legalism in the face of the Gospel ability to meet each man at the level of his need. The Pauline injunction to bear each other's burdens never expires (Gal 6:2).[15]

Robert Kreider in "Brotherly Discipline by the Early Swiss" says, "Anabaptists viewed the true church as a disciplined brotherhood . . . In first-generation Anabaptism one sees no advocacy of brittle, rigid avoidance. . . . Discipline was a part of the whole fabric of brotherhood living, which included continuous nurture, corporate Bible study, mutual aid, mutual admonition."[16]

Cornelius Krahn on "Menno and Discipleship" says,

> It is along the demarcation line between the body of believers and the sinful world that church discipline becomes necessary. Only where there is no distinction between the church and the world is there no church discipline. Discipleship and discipline were inseparable [for Menno]. . . . A follower of Christ disciplines himself under the guidance of the Spirit within the fellowship of Christ.[17]

Marvin Ewert, in "Personality and Discipline" holds that

> Discipline in the life of the church is necessary for a ministry of redemption. Every organization must maintain an inner unity and integrity and set certain limits on the qualifications of its membership. These lines are not set arbitrarily but are directly related to the purposes and functions of the organization. If the church aims to proclaim the Gospel and lead men into holy living, it must deal

---

15. Dyck, "Early Ideas," 54–55.
16. Kreider, "Brotherly Discipline," 57, 59.
17. Krahn, "Menno and Discipleship," 63, 65.

with those persons and influences within its own group which do not contribute to reaching these goals.[18]

It is his assumption that the church tends to focus so much on the end product of redemption "that we lose sight of how people are led or guided . . . to receive the redemptive powers of God into their hearts and lives. . . . Discipline can be redemptive only when the person in need experiences understanding and acceptance."[19] Although sin must be faced and dealt with, "To take an attitude of understanding and acceptance means, though, that we do not heap judgment and condemnation upon the wrongdoer. . . . The task of those who would be instrumental in redemptive and restorative discipline is to create an atmosphere—a relationship—in which the sinner is free to face his condemnation and repent."[20] He speaks of "man in bondage" with unconscious forces binding people to do what they do. Since man cannot "jump out of his skin" we must deal with people at various levels in order to be truly redemptive.

A. E. Kreider in "Standards with Love" summarizes his own paper by saying, "Discipline is needed in maintaining a strong, vital, pure, church. A true church has standards of life, faith, and conduct based on the Bible. The Spirit back of all discipline is love."[21]

The section on "Practice" deals largely with specific areas which are all tremendous fields in themselves. The chapter on "Marriage and Divorce," for example, by Henry Poettcker, is a helpful compilation of thinking on this question together with the writer's own intense biblical study particularly of the significant words. The writer advocates positive and wholesome instruction on the basic meaning of marriage as the major task of discipline. With regard to the knotty question of remarriage, the writer concludes that the New Testament gives no statement permitting remarriage after divorce and that some passages definitely prohibit such remarriage. While the writer seems to recommend this approach to the church and also to have the church show forth genuine forgiveness, he does not really harmonize how the church can really do this.

Rather than commenting further on any other specific problem areas, let us look briefly at the big question with which Jacob T. Friesen deals: "Where do we begin" if we want to become more of a disciplined

18. Ewert, "Personality and Discipline," 97–98.
19. Ewert, "Personality and Discipline," 98.
20. Ewert, "Personality and Discipline," 98, 100.
21. Kreider, "Standards with Love," 112.

brotherhood of believers? Friesen endeavors to take a realistic approach of beginning from where the congregation is, rather than advocating any logical following through of implications with regard to discipline or looking for "a magic wand to transform the local church into a community of believers without spot or wrinkle."[22]

It is pointed out that every genuine renewal of the church in history has been accompanied by vigorous searching of the Scriptures. It is pointed out also that the study of the Scriptures should take place with a "brother," that this is basic in the brotherhood concept of the church and understanding of Scripture.

As C. J. Dyck and Marvin Ewert, Jacob T. Friesen endeavors to learn from psychology and in line with the believers' church concept endorses particularly the principle that personality develops in community rather than in isolation, that is, interpersonal relations. "Now if a person becomes a person by virtue of growing and learning within a human community, it may be said that the Christian becomes what he is by growing and learning within the Christian community. . . . In fellowship persons interact, affect one another for good or ill, build each other up or tear each other down."[23]

Friesen advocates more study by the congregation on the meaning of membership and even suggests that to retain a "live" church membership, individuals be asked to publicly reaffirm perhaps every five years, their belief and personal conviction as members of the church. Communion is to be observed as a time of spiritual renewal and deepening of the fellowship and may even serve as a time to awaken those who come ill-prepared. But we believe exclusion from communion because of persistence in sin would appear a misplacement of the extreme measures of church discipline."[24]

One dynamic which is essential to good discipline is promoting more face-to-face relationships in the church. In larger congregations this may be necessary by emphasis upon "personal groups." These, promoted with understanding, are a way of providing for the more intense personal fellowship and thus a formative and corrective discipline which the larger congregations cannot provide as such.

Other guideposts advocated by Friesen are beginning with the faithful in the church, dealing promptly and personally and as "two friends together" with the offender, preferably by concerned members rather than by church

---

22. Friesen, "Where Do We Begin?," 120.
23. Friesen, "Where Do We Begin?," 119.
24. Friesen, "Where Do We Begin?," 123.

officials. Where these efforts do not succeed, it should become a matter of congregational prayer and searching rather than immediate stern steps.

From the book, particularly the first half, one can make the following general observations:

1. Writers are making a deliberate effort not only to redeem the word "discipline," but to discover the dynamic of redemptive church discipline. Here is a contribution not to be minimized.

2. Discipline grows out of a church concept of the gathered fellowship of disciples. The basic responsibility and vitality of discipline must rest with the local congregation. The sourcebook in itself, however, is evidence that this should be combined with a sharing process in the larger fellowship of congregations.

3. References to the "pure church" are strikingly rare. This is apparently a reaction against the impersonal and legalistic value that has sometimes been placed on the church as an institution. On the other hand there is a very obvious search for the meaning of love and the redemptive fellowship. A unique dimension for this type of Mennonite writing is not only the sensitivity to the individual as such but also what we can learn from psychology by way of helping people from where they are, consciously and unconsciously. Involved also is a challenge to those who are on the leading and disciplining aspect in a particular situation to search their own deeper motivations.

4. Although some may be disappointed, others will be refreshed and challenged by these writings to realize that we do not have easy answers, or answers which can simply be kept intact from one generation to the other. In this connection, also, one appreciates the frank recognition that our appeal to Scriptures as being the sole guide needs to be examined rather carefully in the light of actual church practice over the years. One suspects however that many readers will tend not to struggle through such aspects in C. J. Dyck's paper.

5. It is also clear that discipline is not the means to church revival. It is not a substitute for individual Christian experience and the work of the Holy Spirit in the congregation. As A. E. Kreider says, "The presence of the Holy Spirit in the lives of fellow believers makes discipline

possible in the local church. . . . This conviction gives discipline a spiritual character. . . . Discipline is so largely an inner work."[25]

6. Most writers in the book would apparently agree to an increased emphasis upon self-discipline, more instruction, and seeking to make the church more of a face-to-face fellowship experience. Some would probably not want to go further in clear dealing with individuals who have overstepped limits required or recommended by the congregation. Others would want to work with the individual but not consider excommunication. One must also face the question of whether the local church waits until it reaches a certain level of brotherhood before it carries the discipline process from nurture to admonition and counsel to the sterner measure of excommunication. This is not met sufficiently by any writer.

Studies in Church Discipline is a unique contribution to Mennonite writings. How effective it will be in the process of reversing the sect-cycle once again toward the brotherhood church, will depend on what happens in the local congregation. It is the sincere prayer of this reviewer that many local groups will study this book, honestly look at themselves, and, under the guidance of the Spirit, have the courage to experiment in their congregations.

---

25. Kreider, "Standards with Love," 110.

12

Some Neglected Aspects in the Biblical View of the Church

William Klassen

Rapid strides have been taken in the study of the church in the past sixty years. These studies have moved from the pole of Sohm where everything that takes on form is considered Old Catholic and therefore not in harmony with the original intent of Christ (the ideal church being the charismatic church without structure or legal order) to the opposite pole where the main intent and ideal of the church is a smoothly operating organization. Whether this be the somewhat magical view of the sacraments and preaching which one finds in some of European Protestantism, or the well-oiled, activistic machinery of the American church deriving most of its stimulus (on the local level) from an eager-beaver pastor trying to get ahead and from junior executives on national church boards, makes little difference in the end result. The latter looks with contempt upon theological reflection, hence has never been defended in any detailed fashion.

Much of this interest in the church was fostered by the ecumenical movement, and while there always exists the danger that too much reflection results in sterility, this does not appear to be an acute problem in America and the thought given to the nature of the church has been most productive in renewing its sense of mission and destiny. But we wish to raise some questions:

What Constitutes a Church?

One of the questions on which there continues to be basic disagreement between us and much of the larger Protestant discussion on the church is the question, Who belongs to the church? Lest we become ensnarled in a merely theoretical discussion of the question, Where is the church? it should be observed that it has tremendous repercussions in the actual life of the church. For Luther only two things are really necessary: the proclamation of the Word and the administration of the sacraments rightly according to the gospel. Calvin added the element of hearing of the word which tends to place more emphasis on obedience. Two major Anabaptists, Menno Simons and Pilgram Marpeck, accept this definition of the church in a formal way, but part ways drastically in their definition of what it means to "rightly" administer the sacraments. Believers' baptism and the believers' church are an integral part of the Anabaptist-Mennonite view of the church because it is felt that for the church truly to respond to the lordship of Christ inclusion in his body through baptism must be a conscious response of the individual. The church is a *community of response* and by the very nature of the case this response has to be made by the individual and not by his parents.

Luther also wanted a believers' church, as is often pointed out. This made the problem of faith central for him. While agreeing with Luther that faith is basically a gift of God it is clear that faith without obedience is a contradiction in terms. At this point the Anabaptists registered a protest which is essentially valid.

It is a sad commentary on some contemporary biblical theology that it must continue the rather tendentious hermeneutics of the Reformation and see the element of continuity in the Old and New Testaments in the circumcision-baptism analogy. It is surprising that when the New Testament discusses the element of continuity between it and the Old it mentions "faith" (Heb 11) and that not in the sense of enjoying God's free offer of grace but rather "By faith Abraham . . . obeyed." The Old Testament record shows clearly that when Abraham did not obey, when he substituted his own scheme and plan and lacked confidence in God's covenant, he paid the price. It is on this deeper level that the continuity of God's people is to be sought rather than on the analogy of age in baptism-circumcision. Bishop Fidus who insisted that infant baptism must take place on the eighth day since in that way the circumcision analogy would be carried out was at least consistent, even though Cyprian and the Council of Carthage (251 or 253) won the argument, making baptism mandatory soon after birth.

The basic question is not historical (Did the early church practice infant baptism?) but exegetical and theological. Exegetically Roman Catholic scholars and some Reformed scholars have freely admitted that the New Testament is silent about infant baptism. Others like Cullmann have through some highly imaginative exegesis found it there, but these attempts will not detain us here.

The question that needs to be pressed is: Does the baptism of irresponsible individuals result in a church which is a responsible divine society? If Rom 6 means anything at all, we must conclude that death to sin can only be related to the baptismal experience where the person addressed is aware of his baptismal experience, and where the memory of this great divine act can always guide him in his attitude toward sin. Not only psychological value, but clear theological values spring from the ability to say at every time: "I know when I took the decisive step and responded to God by renouncing the world, the flesh, and the devil—when I died to sin and was raised in newness of life, and that was the hour of my baptism." Here the analogy of circumcision in the New Testament (as already in the Old) is the real circumcision made without hands, "by putting off the body of flesh" (Col 2:11).

This reinterpretation of circumcision was first proposed in the Old Testament by Jeremiah (Jer 4:4; 6:10; 9:25), and is seen at Qumran where 1QS (Rule of the Community) 5:5 reads: "and men of truth shall circumcise the foreskin of their impure desires and stiff-neckedness in the congregation" and in 5:28 the possibility of a reading which calls those who proceed against a fellow member of the congregation bearing a grudge "uncircumcised of the heart."[1]

The repeated admonitions in the New Testament to "put on" and "put to death" indicate that while baptism does mark a decisive point in one's relationship to Christ and his body, the church, it in no way makes one perfect. To deny this is in effect to deny the lordship of Christ (1 Pet 3:21), for baptism saves us "as a pledge to God proceeding from a clear conscience" (1 Pet 3:21). The context clearly indicates that the same thought structure of Rom 6 is herein view, and it includes the analogy between Christ's death

---

1. Meyer, "περιτέμνω, περιτομή, ἀπερίτμητος," 78–79. It should be noted that the content referenced here for 1QS 5:28 is incorrect in the article; the reference should be to 1QS 5:26.

and that of the sinner who dies to sin and is raised in newness of life. Above all he puts on Christ, and the new life in Christ is in no sense a striving after an ideal of Christ which he distills from the New Testament but allowing Christ to be fully formed within him.

It is one of the oddities of history that the term *sacramentum* when originally applied to baptism involved specifically the aspects of vow and commitment but has today lost that meaning almost entirely, unless it is seen as a proleptic vow made by proxy.

This commitment to Christ in baptism is absolute and total. It brooks no rivals and allows no secondary loyalties to overshadow it. All loyalties to family, nation, or community are seen in view of the absolute loyalty which the Christian has to Christ. It is a loyalty to Christ and not to his church which in the course of history has erred grievously and continues to err. On the other hand, one cannot sharply distinguish between Christ and his church, for as long as we are in history the two must be seen together but not identified.

This aspect of Christ's sovereignty needs to be taken seriously. On the one hand, it must be impressed upon all who join the church that they are thereby submitting to a Lord who is above all other lords. On the other hand, it is our responsibility to point out the idolatrous character of other lords which clamor for the allegiance of people today. Sometimes Mennonites have been rightly accused of being pharisaical in their attitudes toward labor unions. In the light of the New Testament we would ask: Can one belong to Christ and take the vow of allegiance demanded by the Teamsters' Union which reads: "I will render full allegiance to this union and never consent to subordinate its interests to those of any other organization of which I am now or may hereafter become a member?" If so, it would be interesting to know how this can be done. It appears that the difference between this and the cult of emperor worship of the first century is that here you are not explicitly asked to curse Christ.

What About the Practice of Church Discipline?

If the church consists of a community of response, a covenant community where all are united to the Lord by a common covenant, then church discipline becomes a constituent part of that community's life. In spite of solid exegetical treatments of church discipline by men like Rudolf Bohren[2] and

2. Bohren, *Das Problem*.

its necessity as a concomitant to the emerging view of the church, there is marked reluctance to do anything about it because of the extremes to which it has gone in sectarian Protestantism and in Roman Catholicism.

Church discipline is a necessary part of genuine church life. It belongs to its essence. If the Society of Biblical Literature and Exegesis drops members for being in arrears in membership fees, how much more should the church take seriously the failure to comply with the vows of membership taken? The necessity of church discipline, however, goes much deeper than that, namely, it seeks to deal with the ever-continuing presence of sin.

We all admit the presence of sin. Roman Catholics realize the necessity of confession and have their own method of dealing with it. Protestants have on the whole refused to deal with it and in the recent past have been only slightly disturbed that the psychiatrist's couch is fast becoming the Protestant confessional booth for the wealthy. Through the upsurge in interest in pastoral counseling, the pastor often becomes the amateur psychiatrist who tries to remove these problems of guilt by various means.

In the light of the Bible and church history one is forced to raise the question: Are these means of dealing with sin adequate? How does my talking about the past to a pagan psychiatrist relate to the Christian community of which I am a part? The ancient church knew of no private penance or confession. The abuses of the private confessional booth were so great that as Protestants we were justified in discarding it. We have failed, however, to devise a valid substitute.

I should like to propose as a substitute a return to the biblical method of church discipline, which apart from its authority as revelation seems to me to be peculiarly relevant to the needs of the church today. The Bible seems to assume that for the church truly to be the church it must have authority to forgive and retain sins—an authority given to it as a body by Christ himself (John 20:20; Matt 18:15). This aspect of the church has not received the attention it deserves, even though it is by no means absent from the New Testament and has been discussed to some extent in exegetical literature. By looking at a specific passage of Scripture we may be guided in our understanding of what it means to be a disciplined community. Matt 18:15–20 lends itself well to such an examination.

The first step is the encounter between the two individuals. If this is fruitless, then an official visit is made by two or three witnesses, and again if the effort is fruitless, the matter goes to the church. By taking two or three along a personal peeve is ruled out, and by referring the matter to the church the danger of a clique ganging up on an innocent victim is circumvented. But Jesus is also realistically aware that even these three steps may stop short of the redemption of the individual and he recommends drastic action to portray to the offender that he is considered no longer a part of the group but considered a tax collector and a gentile. By this he likely means that one begins with him simply as though he had never become a disciple. Through the context of this passage it is clear that the approach is thoroughly redemptive. The church deals with sin—by its very nature it must—but it never sits back in complacent self-satisfaction complimenting itself that it has just rid itself of one of its more undesirable members. It seeks always to win the erring member to a restored fellowship with Christ and his body, the church.

It is the paradox of the church that a group of erring individuals discipline other erring members. But at this point the gospel does not maintain that only a perfect church can discipline. Rather, it insists that the risen Christ moves among his churches and, working through his members, rebukes sin, purges his church, and forgives.

This point is developed well by Bohren. This makes it possible for Paul to advocate the approach he does in 2 Thess 3:6 and 14 where the words, "keep away from any brother" and "have nothing to do with him," indicate a drastic change in relationship which will leave no doubt in the mind of the brother. However, the note of tenderness also pervades this passage: verse 6—"brother"; verse 15—"Do not look on him as an enemy but warn him as a brother."

It is in this context that Jesus promises to be present among his members if they gather in his name, and he surely has reference to the two or three who gather to reprove the erring, and to the church which meets to reprove sins and to forgive. In John 20:23 the forgiveness and retention of the sins is intimately related with the gift of the Holy Spirit. The presence of the risen Christ and the Holy Spirit safeguards the church from condemning as sins those things which are merely cultural practices and should also safeguard it from turning the church into a Jesuitical inquisition.

The context of this pericope is enlightening. The admonition to deal with sin in the brotherhood is reinforced by the solemn assertion, "Verily, I say to you," and the promise already given to Peter in Matt 16 that whatever the disciples will bind on earth will stand bound in heaven, and whatever they will loose on earth will remain loosed in heaven. We should not remove the edge from these sayings by referring to the empirical situation. It was in the presence of Peter's faults that this promise was initially made to him, and it continues to be a part of the life of the church regardless of how imperfect its actual experience within the world may be. The fact is that the church here is given authority to loose and to bind, power which involves forgiving and retaining sins, authority which has its counterpart in heaven and is valid in its courts.

Thus, the corporate church takes the responsibility for the sins of each individual (1 Thess 5:11, 15; 1 Cor 5:2) and the individual carries responsibility for all his brethren (Gal 6:1; 1 John 5:16). Each individual therefore has the authority of Jesus to correct and to convict sins as indeed the Holy Spirit is described in John 16:8, a work which continues at all times in the church. Every disciple of Christ has a word from God which must be heard by his brother. This word is both conviction and forgiveness. What is said of Peter in Matt 16:19 is promised to all the disciples in Matt 18, as in John 20:23 it is promised to all the apostles. As New Testament scholar Julius Schniewind has observed, this is utterly new. No one in Judaism could be certain of his salvation, much less could he promise forgiveness of sins to another. When Jesus does this (Matt 9:2, parr.), this can only mean that he has a share of God's own authority. Moreover, Jesus hands this highest authority down to his church. The power of the binding and loosing word is given to all Christians. Paul presupposes that to receive the word of God is also to give it on to others (1 Thess 1:5–8; Rom 10:8–10) and according to Schniewind there is no basic difference in the Christian church between the one who proclaims the word and the one who receives the word, just as also there is no basic difference between the word which is directed to the whole church and the individual person.

What is it that keeps this from degenerating into a community where human standards of good and evil rule and where discipline becomes a matter of social pressures and individual whims? The guarantee is the promise of Christ's presence. The nature of the formal requirement, namely, that you must encounter the brother and then the brethren, is also a safeguard. To be sure, the church is a fusion of transcendental and immanental factors, but its immanental factors dare never obscure the fact of the divine presence and the action which results in harmony with this presence. It is not without significance that in this context the promise that if two or three agree on earth about anything they ask, it will be done for them by my Father in heaven is expressed (note the parallel passage in John 16:23). This surely means that the binding and loosing must be carried out only in the context of prayer. Beyond this it is noteworthy that the power of prayer rests in the immediate presence of Christ who is the head of his church and active in it at all times. It is striking how in the early church the consciousness of the presence of the risen Christ attended every important event. As Schniewind states: "All that was spoken, done, suffered in the church is word, deed, suffering of Christ."

The necessity of discipline derives from the central core of normative confessional material vitally related to the primitive Christian church and which makes it essential to distinguish truth from error (1 John 4). In its most primitive form this confession was simply "Jesus is Lord" (1 Cor 12:3), but here again its content was related to the historic Christ.

Paul evidences a similar attitude toward church discipline in the Corinthian correspondence. The incestuous man is to be removed from them, but this is an action which requires the assembly, and Paul will be present in spirit, and then "with the power of . . . [the] Lord Jesus, you are to deliver this man to Satan for the destruction of the flesh, that his spirit may be saved in the day of the Lord Jesus" (1 Cor 5:4–5). In 1 Tim 1:20 Paul refers to Alexander and Hymenaeus "whom I have delivered unto Satan, that they may learn not to blaspheme." Whatever the precise connotation of this statement, it is clear that Paul insists that the church (either in body, or by its apostolic leadership) do something about the presence of sin in the group. The goal is the ultimate salvation of the transgressor, but in the meantime no words are spared to make it clear to the individual that he is officially transferred from Christ's kingdom to the domain of Satan. Is this not, in the end analysis, a more redemptive attitude than that so often taken by the modern church in which sin is winked at, gossiped about, but never really rebuked and reproved?

The church needs to be a community of discipline and it must have the experience of declaring forgiveness. This means that it dare not limit its experience to a liturgy read together; meaningful as that may be, it cannot be satisfied with the words of absolution spoken by the minister, valuable as that may be, but it must gather together in small enough groups to make it feasible to share with one another the deepest hurts which we carry around, and assure each other of fullest and freest forgiveness. To turn this experience over to group psychotherapy is to betray our Lord. Group psychotherapy undoubtedly has an important place, but if the church were true to its mission this might be a much more modest place.

PART II: ON COMMUNAL AUTHORITY, "ORDER," AND DISCIPLINE

A word must yet be said about the relation of church discipline to the sacraments. If the position of baptism is in the nature of a service of commitment when the person takes his place in the people of God, then it is obvious that the Lord's Supper in some sense indicates that we have kept our trust with our Lord. This does not mean that we have lived perfect lives, but it does mean that we have examined ourselves and found our basic relationship toward Christ to be one of obedience. To have the flagrant sinner appear at the communion service is to mar the aspect of fellowship which is so central to the service. Unless the meal becomes a service where we receive strength as we imbibe the potion of immortality, we will always need to stress a measure of self-examination. Sharing the cup means that we share our deepest being with someone.

Again, we think of Ambrose, and we recoil. We dare not use the Lord's cup to whip into line a politician who disagrees with the church. But is the prostitution of the Lord's Supper by Ambrose any worse than our own where it is served at the front of the church on a help yourself basis? Rabbi Duncan was right when he encouraged a Highland woman who was weeping to take the sacrament with the words: "Take it; it's for sinners." But we are not right in saying that it is for unrepentant, hardened sinners who are self-satisfied in their sins. By doing so we cheapen the life that was laid down for us—and allow them to drink damnation unto themselves.

Moreover, the practice of church discipline is related to the total worship of the church. This point is made strongly by C. E. B. Cranfield (a Presbyterian) and he deserves to be quoted:

> The proper accomplishment of the human action of worship necessarily involves church discipline. If the church is truly and sincerely responding to Christ's presence in Word and Sacraments and in the persons of His brethren, it cannot help being concerned about the honor of Christ, the conversion of those outside, and the true welfare of its own members. Church discipline is the practical expression of those three concerns.... In insisting on the need for discipline we are not suggesting that the church should attempt to put the clock back and restore discipline as it was exercised in any particular period of the past. Attempts at reformation by simply putting the clock back are apt to be disastrous. But we are suggesting that the whole worship of the main churches of Christendom is today seriously impaired and disfigured by the widespread breakdown of church discipline.[3]

---

3. Cranfield, "Divine and Human," 396.

If, as Cranfield suggests, worship has both the human and the divine element, then he surely is correct in asserting that serious consequences will follow from human delinquency. Nor will the beauty of a pleasing liturgy compensate for a life that is lived in filth.

What Is the Mission of the Church?

Franklin Littell claims that "the Anabaptists were among the first to make the (Great) Commission binding upon all church members." In varying degrees through outside influences our Mennonite churches have recaptured this vision which was literally persecuted out of the original Anabaptists. Surely, we would all agree that in the preaching and teaching ministry of the church moving across the world lies the real mission of the church. The church does not realize its mission when the morning worship "goes off with precision," but the true test of the church comes when men respond to the lordship of Christ. With it comes a life where deed and word coalesce to form one unified witness. If this was the genius of Anabaptism, more's the tragedy that in later years discipline overshadowed the mission of the church. The desire for the faithful church must always go hand in hand with being a witnessing community. The church is a witnessing community and anything which mars its testimony must be taken with utmost seriousness. Its very nature as a people of God emphasizes its relationship to God and its cohesiveness as a people.

An awareness of being the people of God forces a distinction between them and those who do not belong to the people. They are always "a people dwelling alone, and not reckoning itself among the nations" (Num 23:9). The prophet Malachi awaits the day when "once more you shall distinguish between the righteous and the wicked, between one who serves God and one who does not serve him" (Mal 3:18). The report of the 171st General Assembly of the United Presbyterian Church in May 1959 reminded us that in our day "There is not a sufficient discernible difference between the goals, purposes, morals, and aspirations of the average church member and those of his non-Christian friends." This is the constant threat of the church. "The twofold temptation of the church remains the same throughout the centuries: the temptation to conform to the world—the salt losing its savor, therefore useless; and the temptation to live in self-centered isolation—the salt kept in a salt bag, again useless."[4]

4. De Dietrich, *Witnessing Community*, 179.

Franklin Littell observes that "in Biblical living the tension between the 'church' and the 'world' is progressively overcome by the evangelical outreach of the community. The people of the Covenant are a special people, a royal priesthood (1 Pet 2:9) with a special mission and responsibility for those who dwell in darkness."[5] Accordingly, the church discharges its responsibility to the world by evangelizing it and drawing people into the church.

It is not difficult to see that the church's sense of mission can easily be lost by becoming so engrossed in cultivating its own garden that it loses sight of the needs on the outside. Likewise, by sheer force of habit it is treacherously easy to let the sense of mission slip away as the consciousness and conviction of being the people of God fades into unreality and the church settles down to become simply another human society which claims man's loyalty.

All of this directly affects the church's witness. We have heard far too much about the way in which the biblical ethic is bound to its time and have not taken seriously enough the strategy and content of this ethic. If Cullmann is right in asserting that the New Testament views the lordship of Christ as directly over the church and indirectly over the state, then G. Caird is correct in pressing the implications of this for Christian ethics as being much more relevant than is assumed by a large proportion of theologians today. This means that we do not need to divorce Rom 12 from 13 or discard the Christian ethic at the outset and base our witness on a prudential ethic concocted at Broadway and 120th Street, New York. Surely the fact that at the core of Christ's message stands the political term "kingdom," taken with the frequency with which such terms as assembly, people, citizenship, and other political terms occur in the New Testament, is not without relevance for our understanding of the Christian witness to the world within which he lives. Nevertheless, it should be pointed out that the New Testament does not evaluate a witness by its immediate result. The clue to world history is the suffering servant in Deutero-Isaiah and only the lamb standing as slain can break the seals of history in the Apocalypse. The New Testament speaks more about being faithful than relevant, although it certainly does not view these two as being mutually exclusive.

It may be well to cast a glance backward to see what we have tried to establish and to attempt to sharpen the issues before concluding. To the age-old question: What is the church? we have replied that the church is there where Christ is among his people; a people who have responded to

---

5. Littell, *Anabaptist View*, 136.

Christ's call to discipleship. They have been united with Christ. The church is composed of believers who have submitted to the lordship of Christ—not completely to be sure—but nevertheless they are progressively "[destroying] arguments and every proud obstacle to the knowledge of God, and . . . [taking] every thought captive to obey Christ" (2 Cor 10:5). In view of this we marvel that Karl Barth's critique of infant baptism has not been taken more seriously. But we observed also that infant baptism is only one of many ways in which the value of responsible church membership is lost. This leads us to a discussion of church discipline and its importance in the life of the church. Exegetically it was noted that there is strong support for the practice, and it has always been more or less a part of the church's doctrine. However, a large chasm separated the church's belief and its practice at this point. Sometimes discipline concentrates on excommunication, while the New Testament seems to concentrate on restoring a sinner; sometimes it is asserted that the church lacks authority to discipline since we are all sinners. Both of these practices are merely a masquerade for a deeper lack, namely, the conviction that we are the body of Christ and that as we worship, Christ is as clearly in our midst as he was in the assemblies of the early church. We have pointed out that church discipline is valid when biblical, that is, when it is practiced by the group in an attitude of prayer and with the presence of Christ and the Holy Spirit. Unless a church experiences the act of forgiveness it is never the church, and unless it imparts forgiveness to others it fails also to be the church. Scandalous as it may seem this is the record of the church in its greatest period of strength. In this connection a word was said about the place of the Lord's Supper and the place of worship. Finally, a brief look was taken at the church's mission which is seen as proclamation and witness through word and deed. A caution was sounded that we do not evaluate a witness by its immediate results, but rather see it in the light of God's sovereignty over history. Once this is done the church will not be so eager to save its own institutional skin but will be more ready to accept the cross and suffer for its Lord, regardless of the price.

Cranfield suggests that we must think of church discipline in the wider frame of reference, especially the urgent problem of the apartheid policy of the Dutch Reformed churches in South Africa. There is surely a place for such a wider application of church discipline. Certainly in the early church, discipline was practiced far beyond the local congregation as the letters and missionary journeys of Paul make abundantly clear. By speaking to each other, by offering ourselves for correction and conversation, we in effect submit to church discipline.[6]

The question still gnaws: How, on the local level of the church, do we move from theory to practice? It may be suggested that it is impossible to accomplish this without a thorough program of education. Nevertheless, the place to begin would be with those who are now contemplating church membership. By putting some fiber into church membership and uniting it with baptism it could become a deeply moving experience and the adequate symbol of appropriation which F. W. Dillistone finds lacking. Dillistone is quite aware of the problem which the church has inherited by the practice of infant baptism. Church membership is not appropriated. Instead of suggesting that the symbols of the early church have lost their relevance and meaning, perhaps we should seriously consider the biblical emphasis of joining baptism to renunciation and commitment.[7] It could be impressed upon them and those now in the church that being a part of the church means making every decision in the light of Christ's lordship, and that these decisions cannot be made on an individual basis but must be made in interaction with the group. To be sure, all things are pure, but not all things are edifying, and hence the reason for discussion with the brother before an act of any importance is committed. To be concrete: Here is a man who is a member of your congregation and because he is a frugal businessman his employees are the lowest paid in town. His place neither in the local congregation nor in the wider church organization dare affect the action of the congregation. This issue is at least equal in magnitude to that of fornication, but the latter provokes action much more often.

The way to a stronger church life in America is open to us. It cannot be reached, however, through clever satire of the church in suburbia alone. It cannot be reached by adding activities to an already hair-raising schedule. The past centuries have surely taught that it cannot be reached by a retreat from the centers of paganism into cultural enclaves, whether they be in agricultural communities or the ivory towers of a seminary environment. We know too that when Luther relied upon the word and the sacrament to bring into being that church composed of earnest believers for which he yearned, he embarked upon a dead-end road, which especially in his native Germany misfired badly.

6. Cranfield, "Divine and Human," 396–97.
7. Dillistone, "Editorial," 4–7.

It would seem, rather, that modern biblical scholars who are reminding us that the biblical patterns may not be as outmoded as we are prone to think may be stabbing us into a more fruitful and vibrant church life. Will we heed? Will we pay the price of losing our pagan individualism and submitting to the discipline of Christ—the Head—and experiencing genuine biblical fellowship? Or will we continue to grow bigger but not better, continually adapting our message to our rancid pagan culture until we will be Christian in name only? However we may answer this question, we cannot ignore it. Christ's call comes to us, frightened as we are with the prospects of the end of the world because we have done so little to show people what it really means to belong to him. He himself offers to lead us and to exercise his lordship over us. Under his banner the rule of Satan can be destroyed, and the church which dwells where the throne of Satan is can be faithful to him who has the sharp two-edged sword, the words of judgment which proceed from his mouth.

Book List

I. Survey of the Study of the Church

Braun, F. M. *Neues Licht auf die Kirche: Die protestantische Kirchendogmatik in ihrer neuesten Entfaltung*. Einsiedeln: Köln, 1946.

Linton, Olof. *Das Problem der Urkirche in der neueren Forschung*. Frankfurt: Minerva, 1957.

Shaw, Joseph Minard. "The Concept of the 'People of God' in Recent Biblical Research." PhD diss., Princeton Theological Seminary, 1958.

II. Mennonite Contributions or Treatments of Anabaptism

Bender, Harold S. "Church." In *The Mennonite Encyclopedia*, edited by Harold S. Bender et al., Vol. 1. Scottdale: Mennonite, 1955.

———. "The Mennonite Conception of the Church and Its Relation to Present Day Needs." *The Mennonite Quarterly Review* 19.2 (1945) 90–100.

General Conference Mennonite Church. *Nature of the Church: Study Conference*. Newton: General Conference Mennonite Church, 1958.

———. *Proceedings of the Study Conference on the Believers' Church held at Mennonite Biblical Seminary, Chicago, Illinois, August 23–25, 1955*. Newton: General Conference Mennonite Church, 1955.

Littell, Frank H. *The Anabaptist View of the Church*. Boston: Beacon, 1957.

PART II: ON COMMUNAL AUTHORITY, "ORDER," AND DISCIPLINE

III. General Treatments.

Bohren, Rudolf. *Das Problem der Kirchenzucht im Neuen Testament*. Zurich: Zollikon, 1952.
Shelly, Maynard, ed. *Studies in Church Discipline*. Newton: Mennonite, 1955.
Caird, George B. *Principalities and Powers*. Oxford: Clarendon, 1956.
Cranfield, C. E. B. "Divine and Human Action: The Biblical Concept of Worship." *Interpretation* 12.4 (1958) 387–98.
Cullmann, Oscar. "The Kingship of Christ and the Church in the New Testament." In *The Early Church: Studies in Early Church History and Theology*, 105–37. Philadelphia: Westminster, 1956.
Dahl, Nils A. *Das Volk Gottes*. Oslo: J. Dybwad, 1941.
Dillistone, Frederick W. "Editorial: Evangelical Symbolism." *Theology Today* 19.1 (1959) 1–10.
Welch, Claude. *The Reality of the Church*. New York: Scribner's, 1958.

13

Postulates Concerning Religious Intentional Ethnic Groups

CALVIN REDEKOP

It is becoming increasingly apparent that religious sectarian groups are laboring under difficult or even contradictory orientations. These groups operate as it were, within a schizoid framework. This essay will be an attempt to bring out the tensions existing in those groups which adhere to the typical intentional disciplined Church orientation.

The term "Religious Intentional Ethnic Groups" has been adopted for the following analytical reasons: There are many groups which are ethnic, but do not have religious objectives. There are also many groups which are ethnic, but not intentional (thus for example the Poles on Chicago's West Side are members of ethnic groups, but they are not pursuing a conscious policy of maintaining a cohesive community). The Old Colony Mennonite Church of Manitoba and Mexico is a religious intentional ethnic community. It is religious because its purpose for existence is a religious world view. It is an intentional community because it desires to maintain its belief system. It is ethnic because the process of preserving this "Weltanschauung" has created a homogeneous religious, cultural, social and psychological group structure.[1]

---

1. A point of clarification needs to be inserted. A major part of the classical definition of the sect has been its voluntary nature. This proposition is, however, very ambiguous. On a group level, the objectives and practices of the sect are volitionally and voluntarily embraced. But on the individual level, a sect member is often given no individual choice or freedom. The individual who joins the sect from the outside fits the classic definition, but the offspring of sect members are no more voluntary than offspring of territorial

PART II: ON COMMUNAL AUTHORITY, "ORDER," AND DISCIPLINE

There are four basic ideas which will be presented. I have decided to refer to them as postulates, for though they are based on substantial sociological knowledge, they are not "laws" in the ultimate sense. To save time, the term "Religious Intentional Ethnic Groups" will be shortened into symbolic term RIEG.

Postulate No. 1

The more refined and crystallized the world view of a RIEG is and the more socially cohesive it is, the more it differentiates itself from others beyond the group. Spelled out, this means: a) the more it will conceive of itself as orthodox, and consider other groups and people beyond the pale of legitimacy; b) the more infiltration from the outside appears as a threat which may destroy its sense of identity; c) the more a uniform social system emerges with rigid authoritarian control. Closeness demands efficiency and a harmonic division of labor, if the group is to survive.

Discussion: Section "a" is both logically and empirically derived. Dividing sheep from goats is much more difficult than separating turtles from elephants. A juvenile author might paraphrase the relations between RIEG groups and the outside world by staging a conversation among goats and elephants. "We goats certainly don't have much objective assurance that we are different from those woolly neighbors of ours," while the elephants might say, "We elephants are certainly a species by ourselves, look at the differences between us and those poor creeping turtles."

Empirically, the Old Colony substantiates the postulate. They consider themselves "the Church" and all others are "the World." For assuring evidence of this belief, they point to the great differences in belief and behavior that separate themselves from the "goats."

Section "b" is again based on logic and observation. The more homogeneous a group is, the greater a foreign element is visible and injurious. There is no mission work in the Old Colony. Upon questioning, the reasons for lack of outreach included: Why should we engage in mission work? Our children join the church. Why should we want the "world" in the church? All they could do would be to bring in strange beliefs and practices which would undermine our beliefs and unity.

---

church members. There is not enough space here to discuss the dynamics of the voluntary-involuntary nature of the sect.

Section "c": High cohesion of beliefs and outside threats create authority. Outside threats to belief create an increased interdependence (cohesion) and high cohesion creates conformity and uniformity. Uniformity invites control, and control is often couched in certain offices. Authority is thus a mechanism to cope most efficiently with outside threats. Authority thus varies directly with the strength for dissolution or corrosion from the outside.

The Old Colony evidences high uniformity and rigid authoritarianism. Pressures for assimilation from the outside (which are ever present) create uniformity, and authority emerges as the most efficient response to withstand the danger. For example, rubber tires on tractors threaten the breakdown of the group, for then young people could use them to "tear off to the towns." Thus, to meet the threat, a uniform response emerged, namely, to have no tires on tractors. This has been enforced by strong authority, so that deviants are excommunicated by those in authority and this action is supported by lay action through the ban.

Postulate No. 2

The less contact a RIEG has with other groups and people, the more it will develop unique behavior patterns. The following things will result: a) the more the patterns will be considered legitimate and sacred; b) the more difficult change in these patterns becomes; c) the more "holding the line" becomes a value in itself.

Discussion: Section "a" is based on our knowledge of ethnocentrism. The less we know of other alternative patterns of behavior, the more our own is considered universal and sacred. The Old Colony member can hardly believe that there are Mennonites who do not belong to the Old Colony. They cannot believe that a person can be a Mennonite and not dress and behave as they do.

Section "b": This postulate is based on the process of learning itself, and on the function of habit to maintain social integration. In RIEG change of patterns is practically nil, for other patterns are not introduced, or allowed to interfere. Thus, a habit will continue until it is disturbed. Since learning comes from the disturbing of habit, it will practically disappear. The Old Colony offers abundant illustrations of this principle. The introduction of a new idea or practice such as the corn silo came very hard. Even after it had been proven superior economically, some still resisted it on the grounds that it will rot the cow's teeth, shorten the life of the cow, or produce poor milk.

Section "c" is based on the fact that change is disruptive. Since diffusion of new ideas is cut off by isolation, change is not likely to appear. If it does, it threatens the equilibrium of the group. Change from within is less disruptive. The disruptive element in change is mainly its arbitrariness. For example, rubber rims on the buggies were finally allowed after a long struggle which created many factions. Most people felt that it had been better for the issue not to have appeared, for many hard feelings were created, even when the issue was academic. Rubber rims did not involve a principle directly. Rubber rims on buggies was not the real issue. The real issue is keeping the young people in the church, and these "arbitrary" changes in the long run will bring the colony closer to the world, and ultimately entice the young people out. Thus, they say that though the changes are arbitrary, they bring us closer to an undesired goal.

Postulate No. 3

The more closed a RIEG becomes the more it is concerned with the socialization process (socialization refers to the process whereby the preceding generation is able to transfer all the beliefs, goals and behavior of a particular culture to the offspring). This postulate takes the following form: a) we can readily assume that group perpetuation or persistence through time is the goal of most groups. We saw under Postulate No. 1 that mission work is dangerous. Thus the only way to perpetuate the group is to make captive converts of the offspring; b) making converts of the offspring is easy if the formal education system is closed so that no ideas from the outside will enter to contaminate the minds of the plastic youth; c) the socialization process is aided not only by the formal system but by the total impact of the group's culture. There is only one worldview, namely that of the RIEG (it is in this context that voluntary membership for the sect member becomes a misunderstanding).

Discussion: Section "a" needs no theoretical explanation, for it is self-evident. Empirically, the Old Colony provides substantiation in many ways. The functional proof that the socialization process is very real is the fact that almost one hundred percent of the offspring stay in the colonies and accept the values and goals of the church.

Section "b" follows logically. If transmitting certain things is important, means will be devised to do this, and they will be rigidly controlled. The school system of the Old Colony is very closely watched. It is under the direct supervision and guidance of the bishops and ministers. The exodus from Russia to Canada and from Canada to Mexico was in the main made because of the threat to the autonomous control of the schools. Reading newspapers and books is frowned upon. No books are allowed in the schools which contain pictures, for the very obvious reason that the closed system of education is betrayed when a glimpse of the outside world is available.

Knowledge concerning section "c" has emerged through the study of symbolic logic and the sociology of knowledge. The anthropological approach to cultures and subcultures has produced firm evidence of the strength of the total cultural pattern on the character of the individual. This process is observable in the Old Colony. The ethnocentric worldview is so deeply and completely ingrained that it is inconceivable to the Old Colony that another way of life could be possible or desirable. The only dissatisfaction I found was the difficult economic struggle. But this reinforces the argument, because hardship might have produced discontent and disloyalty, but I found none. They talk instead of moving to that promised land where they will be allowed to perpetuate their way of life without interference, and where the economic struggle would be less severe. This ethnocentric philosophy is best described by a term they use, namely "the world." By "the world" they mean everything which does not pertain to their experience.

Postulate No. 4

The preceding postulates point to an inclusive postulate which has serious implications for Christian groups that stress cohesive relations and close discipline (RIEG tendencies). The postulate is as follows: The more a religious group stresses the externally disciplined brotherhood, the more it will be plagued by the ethnic postulates outlined above. Conversely, the more a religious group stresses an individualistic personal relationship, the more it will tend to lack discipline, but succeed in outreach and perpetuation of its beliefs. There are thus two opposite poles toward which religious groups will gravitate. Those groups which, however, adhere to both of these poles (or at least intend to) are the ones referred to in the opening paragraph as schizoid.

When a group has RIEG tendencies, it will be less successful in outreach but more successful in maintaining a disciplined fellowship. The group with less RIEG tendencies will be effective in outreach but will lack cohesion and the disciplined brotherhood. It is very probably that the position in between these poles is unstable (i.e., the group will tend to go in either direction but not remain as it intended to). Diagrammatically, the proposition looks as follows:

Type of Group	Resultant Structure
Religious Intentional Ethnic (stress on brotherhood)	Strong discipline, weak outreach
Non-REIG denominations (stress on piety)	Weak discipline, strong outreach
Intermediate position (probably unstable)	Moderate discipline, moderate outreach

Epilogue

The conversation is hopefully not finished. There should be some workable alternative. I believe there is, and this alternative I term the Covenant Community. It is concerned with both objectives, i.e., brotherhood and outreach (discipleship and apostleship) but it is concerned not with perpetuation but with reaching a workable knowledge and faith for one point in time. It realizes that knowledge and understanding are contingent on the forces that are present in a particular context. It believes that there are timeless principles, but these principles need to be accepted and integrated within the times and lives of those making up the community.

14

On Fraternal Admonition

Balthasar Hubmaier

> Where this is lacking, there is certainly also no church, even if Water Baptism and the Supper of Christ are practiced.
> —Dr. Balthasar Hubmaier of Frieburg, Nikolsburg, 1527[1]

Dr. Balthasar Hubmaier was one of the most striking figures in the Reformation of the 1520s. A trained theologian, once vice-rector of the University of Ingolstadt, he was the only Anabaptist to come out of official Roman Catholic intellectual circles. A most gifted and popular preacher, he was in his Catholic days Cathedral preacher at Regensburg and could with his preaching touch off anti-Semitic violence and create a center of Marian pilgrimages.

Expert popularizer, he produced in his "On the Christian Baptism of Believers" (1525) the first and classic tract on baptism, and in his several catechetical and liturgical writings (of which the following is one) translated the concept of the believers' church into the flesh and bones of church order. By far the most prolific Anabaptist writer of the 1520s (nineteen printed works in a little over two years) he has been under-esteemed by Mennonites because of his acceptance of the Sword.

The following text is drawn by permission from a collection of Hubmaier's writings being prepared under the auspices of the Institute of Mennonite Studies.

---

1. Hubmaier, "On Fraternal Admonition," 373.

PART II: ON COMMUNAL AUTHORITY, "ORDER," AND DISCIPLINE

When a people has heard the word of God, accepted it, believed it, committed itself in water baptism to God publicly before the church:

- henceforth to live according to the command of Christ, having promised God to be subject to him and (in the power of God, Father and Son and Holy Spirit) to work and to suffer, in fortune and misfortune, in joy and suffering, in living and dying, yea however God may dispose...

- that it desires to accept all things willingly and with Christ to suffer, die and be buried, in the hope and confidence also to rise again with him by the glory of the Father...

- to walk in newness of life and henceforth not to permit sin to rule in the mortal body, nor to be obedient to its desires, but rather to abandon one's members in obedience to God the Lord to be weapons and an instrument of righteousness that they might be holy and might reach that goal which is eternal life, a gift of God in Christ Jesus our Lord...

- and that they would in eternity jubilate "Holy, Holy, Holy!" and sing to him praise, honor and adoration in eternity.

Yea and when, in public confession of Christian faith, and with the receiving of water baptism, the people has let itself be counted, marked and incorporated in the fellowship of the holy universal Christian church—outside which there is no salvation, as outside the ark of Noah—now out of this people a particular visible congregation has been brought into being. A new daughter has been born to her mother the universal Christian church, which [daughter] now fittingly must do the will of her mother, as the mother, i.e., the general Christian church, does the will of her spouse and bridegroom, who is Christ Jesus the Son of the living God, whose will he too did unto the death. So that thereby the will of God the Father will be done on earth as it is in heaven in like fashion by the beloved Son, mother and daughter.

Whereupon, O you believing Christians, it is always necessary, since men are by nature children of wrath, evil, and vicious, to treat them with wholesome medication, and in fact sometimes completely to cut off the corrupt and stinking flesh together with the poisoned and unclean members, so that the entire body might not thereby be deformed, shamed, and destroyed, but rather that Christian men might progress and persevere in their newly

Christian life once begun, and not fall back like a wild sow into the mudholes of sin, back again into the wrath of God. All of which cannot be better achieved otherwise than according to fraternal admonition according to the institution and order of Christ (Matt 18).

Fraternal Admonition

Yea, as God lives and testifies, I tell the truth. Unless fraternal admonition is again restored, accepted, and used according to the earnest behest of Christ, it is not possible that things might proceed aright and stand well among Christians on earth. Even if we should all shout, write, and hear the gospel until we are hoarse and tired, still all shouting, effort, and industry is in vain and useless. Yes, even water baptism and the breaking of bread are vain, pointless, and fruitless, if fraternal admonition and the Christian ban do not accompany them, admonition belonging to baptism as the ban belongs to communion and fellowship.

This we have within a few years clearly seen and evidently experienced in many places. In which time the people had learned no more than two points, without any amelioration of life. The one point, that it could say: "We believe. Faith saves us." Secondly: "We can do nothing good of ourselves." Now both of these are true. But under the mantle of these half-truths all kinds of viciousness, unfaithfulness, and iniquity have completely taken over, and fraternal love has meanwhile become colder among many, more than in many thousand years. Yea, the common proverb is true and is fulfilled: The older, the worse. It is not improving; it is getting worse. The older, the colder. The longer the world stands, the more evil it becomes. And we must accept this slap in the face from the godless.

But—let us lament it before God—we suffer this through our own fault. For we all want to be Christians and good Protestants by taking wives and eating meat, no longer sacrificing, no more fasting, no more praying, but apart from this, one sees nothing but tippling, gluttony, blaspheming, usury, lying, deceit, skinning and scraping, stealing, robbing, burning, gambling, dancing, flattery, loafing, fornication, adultery, rape, tyranny, thuggery, murder. Here all the frivolity and insolence of the flesh finds free play; here the voluptuousness of this world has the place of honor, rules, jubilates, and triumphs in all things.

Here no Christian deeds shine forth among men. Brotherly love and faithfulness are utterly extinct. Yet all of this (as painful as it is to say it) comes to pass behind the facade of the gospel. For as soon as you say to such "Evangelical" people: "Brother, it stands written, forsake evil and do good," immediately he answers, "It stands written, we can do no good. Everything comes to pass according to the providence of God and necessarily."

They mean thereby that sin is permitted them. If you say further, "It stands written, they who do evil shall go into eternal fire," immediately they reach for a fan of fig leaves to cover their vice with, and say, "But it stands written: faith alone saves us and not our works."

Thanks to such devious argument we are after all good evangelicals, and know how to cite, decorate, and embroider holy Scripture like the friends of Job and like the devil (Matt 4)—skillfully and masterfully to cover over the self-willed license and shamelessness of our flesh.

But if fraternal admonition were to be restored among us, such excuses and counterfeit embellishment of our sins and vices would soon be uncovered and made an end to. Let us with the help of God undertake fraternal admonition not only in teaching but also with the hand and deed. Would God graciously accord to us his grace and the power to achieve the same. Then the old Adam will just begin to raise his ears, to grumble, to buck, to snort, and to kick out before and behind.

For he can absolutely not accept such admonition. He wants to be a Christian and yet above being reproached. But in the power of the Holy Spirit, we will show him something quite different and we ask of his inborn pride that he give us a gracious hearing. But in case he should not want to accept this now, he will have to let it happen at the last judgment. Hereby we will have preserved our honor and conscience toward him.

Suppression of Vice

Christ Jesus our Lord and Savior always and in every way brought forth great industry and earnestness in order to uproot and to suppress the vices among his people, by which many men are offended, made more evil, and robbed of eternal life. He says, "Woe to the world because of scandal. Woe, woe to him through whom scandal comes. It were better for him that a millstone were hanged around his neck and he were thrown into the sea than that he should offend one of these little ones. Watch out" (Luke 17). "But if your brother sins against you, go and admonish him between yourself and him alone. If he hears you, you have won your brother" (Matt 18).

Here, Christian reader, in the words "against thee," or "into thee," should be noticed that there are two kinds of sin, public and secret. Public: Those which are committed shamelessly before all men. These sins should be reprimanded also publicly and immediately, so that no one among the pious and simple people may be misled nor seduced and might say, "if it's all right for him, then it's also all right for me"—as the common people have done and lived until now in fornication and all adultery, because they saw that their chaplains and rulers led the same kind of life.

Similarly, as soon as the pope had allowed the spiritless crowd and foundations to take five gulden (and a little more) per hundred, counter to the bride and the clear word of Christ, Luke 6, then others as well have done the same and in fact made a respectable business out of it. Scandal is such an evil sin, it eats away all around itself like cancer and leprosy, if it is not hastily uprooted through fraternal admonition. Wherefore Paul teaches us, writing: "they who sin publicly, prove them before all, so that the others might fear."

Likewise, Christ reprimanded Peter, when he had pled with him in just a few words, in a human and well-intentioned way, that he should take care of himself and not go to Jerusalem so that evil might befall him. Immediately Christ says to him, "Get away from me, Satan, you are a stumbling block to me, for you think not what is godly but what is human."

Similarly, Peter reproves Simon, because he wanted to buy the Holy Spirit from the apostles with money, and says, "May you be damned with your money, for thinking that the gift of God could be purchased with money. You shall have no part or share in this word, for your heart is not sincere before God, so repent of this thy wrongness and pray to God."

Yet let every Christian take heed to himself that such remonstrance and sharpness of the word might flow forth out of love and not from envy, hate, or wrath, as we see in the words of Peter, when he desires the welfare of Simon and says, "repent." In just the same way Paul also reproaches Peter, when he saw that he was not behaving according to the truth of the gospel, and says, "If you, who are a Jew, live as a Gentile, and not Jewishly, why then do you force the Gentiles to live as Jews?" Yes, Paul withstood Peter publicly to the face, because he was reprehensible.

Sins Which Are Private

But some sins are private, which are committed in stillness and hiddenness. Such sins should also according to the command of Christ be reproved privately. Thus, Nathan the prophet reproved King David and Christ reproved Judas the betrayer, in front of the disciples it is true but by a hidden manner of speech. If your brother then hears you, obeys your admonition and forsakes the sin, then with one act you have profited more than all the merchants of Venice in their whole life.

Should he not hear you, then take one or two with you as witnesses. If he will not hear them, then tell it to the congregation, thereby you are doing the will and following the earnest command of Christ, who in one commandment has bound together two salutary commands. Namely, that he first has commanded you to admonish your brother or else you are participant in his sins; but with these same words he has commanded your brother, to accept fraternal admonition from you meekly and honorably. If he does this, so he is whole; if he does not, then you are from this point on innocent before God of his sin.

At this point carnal wisdom (to which all words of God are poison and gall) grumbles and says, "This does not seem right to me, that my brother should make manifest my private sins. He would not want me to do that to him, accordingly he should reasonably also spare me the same and much rather help me to cover over my sins." Answer: This is why he reprimanded you between himself and yourself alone, so that your sin would not become manifest. But you did not want to hear him, therefore according to the command of Christ he had to bring with him two or three, once again hoping to be able to win your soul, so that you might not need to be ashamed before the whole congregation.

When you refused to accept the same, only then did he have to go on and bring it before the church. For the command of Christ and the salvation of your soul were of deeper concern to him than your temporal, false, and hypocritical honor and piety, wishing that you might be considered righteous when you were unrighteous. For it is still much better for you to be shamed in front of a particular congregation than before the church universal and all the heavenly hosts at the last judgment. For what is ever so private will be made public and especially all sin must absolutely be put to shame.

Since then you did not want to hear the church either, then it was better for you that you should be excluded and considered as a pagan, rather than that you would bring to shame the whole church through scandal, and that you might have seduced other members with yourself into sin and eternal perdition. It was also better for you for the reason that you might then come to awareness, recognize your misery, desist from sins, and then you would be received again by the church with great joy and admitted into her Christian communion.

On Accepting Admonition

You see, righteous Christian, how useful and salutary is brotherly admonition to him who recognizes its wholesomeness and who honestly accepts it. Yet flesh, blood, and the soulish man cannot grasp this. He wants ever to be looked on as pious and be reprimanded by no one. But he who is spiritual judges all things. But such admonition and exclusion is not only good for man according to the nature of the case, but it would also be much better for him that a millstone be hung around his neck and he be thrown into the sea than that he should give the very least offense or scandal in the church and pile sin upon sin.

Now since fraternal admonition and the Christian ban proceed from such inner, heartfelt, and fervent love, which one Christian should have daily toward another in true faithfulness, therefore he must be a most ignorant, wild, and godless monster, yea a grim Herod, who would not accept such admonition from his brethren in a friendly and kind way, and with thanksgiving.

One thing more you must know, faithful reader. That in these matters there are two kinds of commandment. The first orders each Christian in particular to admonish his sinning brother according to the order of Christ. The other commands the admonisher, that he must first take the plank out of his own eye in order to be able to see to remove the splinter which is in the eye of his brother.

This is the true order of Christ, which should be practiced just in this way. But the first commandment is not done away with by the second. For it is better to fulfill one commandment than to neglect them both. Therefore no one can be excused who would fail to admonish his brother simply because he himself is a sinner, for in this way brotherly admonition would completely collapse. Rather the greatest sinner of all is obligated to admonish his brother, or else through his silence he makes himself a participant also in the guilt of another.

This is what Isaiah called being companions of thieves (Isa 1:22). David calls it consenting with thieves and partaking with adulterers (Ps 50:18). I say this for this reason: Under the appearance of recognizing that we are all sinners, no one was willing any more to admonish others, nor to accept admonition, and thus fraternal admonition was completely smothered and turned to ashes.

How to Admonish One Another

According to Scripture it shall proceed as follows: Brother! It stands written that men must give an account on the judgment day for every vain word that they have spoken. Now dear brother you made a baptismal pledge to Christ Jesus our Lord. You committed yourself to him in such way, and publicly pledged it before the church, that you would henceforth desire to direct and rule your life according to his Holy Word (to which scripture testifies); and that if you should not do so, you would willingly let yourself be admonished according to the command of Christ. Thereupon you received water baptism and were numbered in the membership of the Christian community.

Now you are using much vain language and frivolous speech, whereby good morals are seriously destroyed, as is not fitting for a Christian man. I therefore remind you of your baptismal pledge, my dearest brother, that you would call to memory what you promised to God, and I beg you for the sake of God and of the salvation of your soul henceforth to avoid such frivolous talk and to improve your life, thus doing the will of God.

If now your brother ceases to sin, you have won a precious jewel. If he does not, then take two or three witnesses with you and try once more in the same words. If he will not hear them either, then say to the congregation, which will know how to proceed. Deal in the same way with all other sins.

If further you notice, Christian man, that one brother has something against another, envy, hate or another kind of enmity, bring them together and hold before them the teaching of Christ, who says, "If you are offering your gift on the altar and there you become aware that your brother has something against you, leave the gift at the altar and go, reconcile yourself first with your brother, then come and offer your gift." For God will not receive or accept anything from us graciously, if we still bear enmity against our neighbor. Thus, reconcile them between yourself and both of them. But if they will not hear you, then proceed as was indicated above with fraternal admonition.

Verily, verily, where this happens, here God will stand powerfully and wonderfully by his word, in such a way that the Christian brethren and the fellowship will be able to reconcile and conciliate such great causes and disunities, which could not have been judged in many years at great cost and with great damage. The party which refuses, the same God will punish with such measure that for ten he will lose one hundred gulden, yea even bodily life. God is so strong that he is peaceful with the peaceable and contentious with the contentious. He can punish contention with contention.

Such exhortation and admonition, Christian brethren, cannot occur in a better way than according to the precedent of the word of God, that is with the Ten Commandments and other Christian teachings. For these things are written, as Paul says, for our exhortation, upon whom the end of the world has come. And elsewhere: All scripture given by God is useful for teaching, for admonition, for betterment, for discipline in righteousness, that a man of God might be unchanging, apt for every good work.

Source of Authority

Now we see clearly whence the authority arises that one brother has the power and the right to admonish another. Namely from the baptismal commitment, which a man gave before receiving water baptism, in which he subjected himself, according to the order of Christ, to the church and all her members. This is something which the antichrist and his troop cannot stand. He claims to be fully infallible, free, and blameless, even if he daily leads a great crowd of souls into hell. Yet no man can say to him: Why do you do thus? For this reason, he has overturned all meaningful baptismal pledge and water baptism itself, because they were unreconcilable with his pride, pomp and avarice. But still he wants to be counted as a baptized Christian in the church, yes in fact to be a head of the church, and cannot accept that anyone would say to him: Brother Pope, Brother Bishop, Brother Kaiser, King, Prince or Lord, you are in error and sinning against God.

This is why the antichrist has day and night put forth such a remarkable effort in order to empty out Christ's water baptism for him and replace it with his counterpart, miserable anti-Christian infant baptism. So that, if someone would faithfully remind him of his sacramental baptismal confession and commitment, he could easily excuse himself by saying, "but I was a child, I didn't understand Latin, I didn't promise anything, nor did I even know then what a pledge, faith, Christ, baptism, or fraternal admonition are." But you anti-Christian crowd, such an excuse will not help you, for the gospel has been preached in all the world as a testimony to you. No one can excuse himself.

He who then will loosen the smallest of the commandments of Christ, he will be the least in the kingdom of heaven. Woe, woe, woe to all those who have dissolved and abused the water baptism of Christ, fraternal admonition, the Lord's Supper, and the Christian ban. They who rightly practice and teach the commands of Christ, blessed, blessed, blessed are they for they will be called great, great in the kingdom of heaven.

What of Sacraments?

So all of those who cry: "Well, what about water baptism? Why all the fuss about the Lord's Supper? They are after all just outward signs! They're nothing but water, bread and wine! Why fight about that?" They have not in their whole life learned enough to know why the signs were instituted by Christ, what they achieve or toward what they should finally be directed, namely to gather a church, to commit oneself publicly to live according to the Word of Christ in faith and brotherly love, and because of sin to subject oneself to fraternal admonition and the Christian ban, and to do all of this with a sacramental oath before the Christian church and all her members, assembled partly in body and completely in spirit, testifying publicly, in the power of God, Father, and Holy Spirit or in the power of our Lord Jesus Christ (which is the same power), and giving one's hand in pledge of faithfulness. Look to this, dear brethren, and not to water, bread or wine, lest our water baptism and breaking bread might also be only an appearance and a sleight-of-hand, nothing better than what the stupid child baptism and child feeding have been before, if fraternal admonition and the Christian ban do not constantly accompany them.

In sum: Where water baptism is not given according to the order of Christ, there it is impossible to accept fraternal admonition from one another in a good spirit. For no one knows either who is in the church and who is outside. No one has authority over another, we are scattered, as sheep without shepherds, without a pasture, without markings, neither knowing nor being able to recognize who has let himself be marked as a sheep of Christ, or who chooses to remain as a wild buck outside the flock of Christ. May God help us all, that we might enter into the sheepfold of Christ through the right door, and not climb in elsewhere, against the express ordering of Christ. Amen.

Truth Is Unkillable

15

Walking Together in East Africa

Don Jacobs

While not claiming for itself much more than the fact that it is a group of sincere believers seeking to live the life of Christ, the East African Revival has become a significant modern movement as a binding and loosing fellowship. Those in the fellowship would be the first to admit that they are simply learners in the experience or rather the experiment of walking together in Christ, and that they furthermore do not presume to attain consistently the perfect unity which they so greatly desire. There are periods of coldness, to be sure, but the revival fellowship has been such an effective factor in the life of the *koinonia* in East Africa for the past thirty years that it bears examination.

Thirty years ago, East Africa presented a rather dismal picture of church life. During the first three decades of this century, church growth was very rapid; so rapid, in fact, that Christian nurture lagged far behind as the harvest was being reaped. This situation produced a type of church life which was more formal than real, more nominal than spiritual, and it became quite clear that church members lacked any real sense of *koinonia*.

The church had taken on many functions normally carried on by the tribal social institution—such as defining morality—but had failed to become a body in which meaningful decision-making could take place. Many people experienced new birth, of this there can be no doubt, but few of them discovered the secret of walking together in the newness of life. Large numbers of baptized Christians lost their rights of communion due to infractions of the rules which were set by the church. This caused serious concern among the leaders of the church, but they were quite helpless to do very much about it.

Attempts Unsuccessful

They did try various methods to lop off the dead wood in order to give the church some vitality but they had very disappointing results. Great efforts were made to define the rules more accurately and to preach and teach with greater vigor. Yet sins of every description permeated the church, not excluding sins among many leaders. There were no significant pockets of holiness in the church community to set a standard for church life.

And to further complicate the picture, those who were in control of church matters, those who were trying desperately to do something about the lethargy in the church, happened to be white missionaries. The local people no doubt felt the frustration of the missionaries, but they probably thought—why get so excited about the infringement of the church rules? And anyway, the church was growing, and the giving was fairly good. What more was desired? At this time there was also a growing reluctance to accept uncritically the views of the missionaries. And in reporting the situation correctly it should be said that the missionaries were probably often expecting a higher standard of Christian conduct among these recent believers than was expected in the congregations from which they had come in the "mother church." It was quite obvious that most of the believers were not taking their Christian profession seriously. In fact, in many instances the acceptance of Christ as Savior did not reach a very significant level of meaning in their lives. Most believers held to two worlds, the new superficial Christian one, and the traditional one which still formed their real community.

This greatly weakened the effectiveness of the church. The church was something foreign and abnormal in the society. But to consider getting rid of it would have been unthinkable because the church stood for progress and general advancement in the community. And after all, was not the church involved in education and medicine, and a host of other activities which could aid one in moving into the new day?

The church had failed to become a community. It was a strange institution proclaiming its sacred nature and mission while living as an island apart.

PART II: ON COMMUNAL AUTHORITY, "ORDER," AND DISCIPLINE

Discovered *Koinonia*

It was in this most unlikely situation that the Holy Spirit began to work to bring about meaningful *koinonia* in the early 1930s. It began in Ruanda, a little backward highland country squeezed in between Tanzania and the Congo. It was there that a little group of Christians who were working together in a hospital came into an experience of meaningful *koinonia* in Christ.

It was a mixed group, both white and black, but was welded together in mutual covenant based upon repentance and a new-found freedom in Christ. This experience was so meaningful to these few people, they felt so much power released in their own lives, that they began to send little teams throughout the countryside to bear witness to the new meaning which they found in Christ and in fellowship together. Almost everywhere these teams went, the reality of Christ in their lives brought conviction of sin in others and people were saved. The repentant people then met together regularly for sharing and mutual edification. This was not carried on in any church structures even though the groups often met in church buildings. These fellowships were drawn geographically rather than denominationally.

This movement grew until today there is a network of fellowship groups which covers all of East Africa. Almost every little hamlet has its small group. These groups keep in touch with each other by letter and also through mutual visitation. In addition, the groups within each district get together regularly and there is usually an annual national convention and occasionally an East African convention. These larger meetings tend to check deviance where it may occur. These large meetings also attract hundreds of unsaved people, many of whom are brought to the Lord through the ministry of these conventions.

Meetings Described

What actually takes place at the local fellowship level? Perhaps a review of the typical form of a meeting would be helpful in answering this question. Meetings usually begin with sharing at the level of spiritual experience. How has Christ been meeting your needs of late? Where has the battle been in your life? What new insights have you received on your pilgrimage? Time does not usually allow for everyone to speak, so sharing in this period is limited to those who have significant recent spiritual experiences which they desire to share.

Needless to say, if the group detects insincerity in a testimony, and they often do, then there is usually but mild enthusiasm registered as a result of it. The group, almost unconsciously, assents to sincere testimony. In fact, when a clear and authentic witness is given, the group often breaks out in spontaneous singing. Following the sharing period, the group turns to the Bible which is expected to speak to their immediate needs individually and corporately. Someone leads out, calling for a Scripture to be read which is then followed by comment and discussion which usually takes the form of a response to the word rather than argument or debate. After the word is heard and applied to life the group joins in prayer.

The final period of the fellowship meeting is then used to share matters concerning the more mundane affairs of life. Travel plans and proposed changes in employment of members, and this sort of thing, are discussed. Sometimes a few people stay behind after the others go to help others with specific problems which may be of a spiritual or of a business nature. Marriage arrangements are, incidentally, made in this way.

Extent of Membership

This fellowship movement does not have members, so to speak, but anyone who has an up-to-date relationship with the Lord is welcome. If a person does not repent about a certain issue when it is obvious that he should do so, the group assists him to see his need and encourages him to repent, to break, not as obedience to a law, but because the group feels that it is discerning the mind of the Spirit for him. If the person does not feel that he has any debt or for some other reason refuses to repent, the group drops the issue for the time being, but he is expected to weigh the matter carefully. He is encouraged to continue to meet with the group in their regular meetings. The group will discern whether his matters have been put right or not by his freedom and power or lack of either or both. They know, furthermore, that time does not take away sin; it is Christ's cleansing which does that.

These groups are quite heterogeneous, including people from many denominations. There is no attempt to pull out of denominational churches, but, on the contrary, the function of the fellowship is to provide a meaningful primary relationship with others who are also sincerely seeking to walk with the Lord every day. It is a fellowship of light and deep mutual concern. These people then serve in their denominational churches as best they can;

they are often the teachers and leaders. This fellowship therefore strengthens the denominational churches.

The significance of this movement for spiritual life in East Africa is beyond question. One wonders what would have become of the churches if these people had not discovered this new mutual meeting place in Christ. Those who are in these groups have indeed discovered the miracle of Christ-centered *koinonia*. They have discovered what to them is an authentic binding and loosing community.

16

Dealing with Other People's Sins[1]

Samuel Shoemaker

What shall we do about other people's sins? If we could get the right answer to that question, I think we could lessen the amount of fresh evil that we all contribute to the world's unhappy life by just about 95 percent.

We meet other people's sins all day long, and the effects of them. Many of life's crises and much of its long-standing misery come from the wrongs that other people do. We are never free from these things as caused by others, and they are never free from them as caused by us. They constitute evil enough without our adding to the evil by taking them in the wrong way.

Sometimes these wrongs touch us directly. A business partner turns out to be sly and dishonest and involves us in his own dishonesties. Another woman comes into the picture and takes a man away from his lawful wife. Someone is left in charge of an estate in which we have an interest, plays fast and loose with its investments, and we lose by it. One could add endlessly to the list. A minister comes in contact with dozens of these wrongs almost every week of his life.

Or these sins of other people may touch those whom we love or for whom we feel responsible. We know a dependent woman with a rascally brother who gets away with the money he was supposed to be taking care of in her behalf. A woman walks out on her husband and children; they are neighbors of ours and we carry a concern for them.

---

1. From Shoemaker, *Extraordinary Living*. Used with permission.

PART II: ON COMMUNAL AUTHORITY, "ORDER," AND DISCIPLINE

Someone makes what we think a bad mistake in relation to our children—a teacher planting atheistic or subversive ideas in their minds, a playmate getting them into some kind of scrape, even a Scout leader or church school teacher taking a line with them which we feel to be mistaken. We are not directly hurt ourselves, but we smart and burn vicariously for wrongs done to other people for whom we feel pity or concern or responsibility.

What attitude should we take? What course should we pursue?

Our Attitudes

Let us think first about some of the attitudes we often do take and the course we begin to pursue, perhaps before we have had time to think.

We are likely to feel first a flash of indignation. We may "hit the roof," as the expression is. We have a ready epithet for people who do as this person has done, and we fit it quickly to him. "That so-and-so, and he's sitting up in church on Sundays and singing hymns as if he weren't a rotten hypocrite from head to foot." If a passing thought comes into our minds that we are not perfect ourselves, we comfort ourselves by saying, "I may not be too good, but at least I don't do that," which puts the other fellow way down and us quite a ways above him.

If someone else breaks in on our moral tirade, we may drop the matter from speech, but go on chewing our cud about it in silence. Or we may come back to it again, saying, "But this is righteous indignation. This really was an awful thing that he did. We must uphold what is right." All of which has some truth and justification in it, but not very much light on how we should meet wrongs done by others.

Then we begin to tell about the wrong. We do not go to the person involved; we go to others who will shake their heads morally with us and exclaim, "Too bad," when they rather enjoy hearing of it.

It gives us a feeling of moral superiority to be condemning someone else. We seem to gain something in stature by putting somebody else down. We want comfort in the sin of condemnation; so we feel people out a little before going into the whole story; and when we feel free to tell it, we bring it all out.

With the telling, it gets worse. By now there are two more sinners adding to the sin of the first one! Now the truth is that nothing is ever gained, and much is often lost, by going to a third person with a tale. It is a sure way of making a bad matter worse. It adds to the weight of sin that the person condemned is already carrying, the added load of still more condemnation. It sets loose in the air negative and unkind emotions. If the third party is no more responsible in handling other people's sins than you are, all this just gets multiplied and spread abroad.

It would be a great and good thing if all who call themselves Christians, and all who work and worship in the church, would seal their own mouths forever from speaking to a third person about anybody's sins. We should save almost all church rows. We should save an immense amount of time spent by ministers and others in trying to heal breaches between people. We should keep our own lives free from one of the most pharisaical and hypocritical of sins, the telling abroad of other people's sins.

Results in Relationships

There are, it seems to me, three attitudes we can take toward other people's sins. We can abjure; we can endure; or we can cure, or at least try to.

When we abjure, we renounce the person. We do not wish to see him. We "keep out of his way," as we say. Some things, we tell ourselves, are not so bad, but this is really too much, we simply cannot be seen with such a person.

I think there is as much guilt and wickedness as you can find anywhere in the kind of church member who withdraws from an alcoholic, especially an unconfessed and unadmitted alcoholic who if the church member really had any humility and faith he ought to be willing to try to help. His withdrawal and detachment of himself from great human need does not point to his own superior goodness; it points to his pride, his Pharisaism, his spiritual powerlessness. Far better, I believe, in God's sight the fellow-drunk who goes to him with what kindness he can take, than the so-called Christian who wraps his skirts about himself and will not be tarnished by the sins of one who now becomes to him an outcast.

When a person has done something to us that we think beyond forgiveness, we no longer make any attempt to repair the relation. We say we forget it—forget him. We sometimes say that such a person is to us as one dead. There are people in many churches who have said that about members of their own family. The trouble is we cannot and do not forget. The memory of that broken relation, and our part in keeping it broken, lies festering in our minds. We think of it persistently, never so much as when we determine not to. When, to the wrong another has done us, we add the wrong of lovelessness and unforgivingness, we compound the sin. We must never forget the wise and profound saying, "It is harder to forgive those whom we have wronged than those who have wronged us." We cannot put people out of our minds. We cannot even do it when they are dead. Nothing puts the wrong out of our minds but righting it.

Sometimes we decide just to endure. There is a husband with a vile temper. The wife did not see it when they were engaged, for he kept it under, but as soon as they were married it began to show itself. She long ago decided to put up with it, and she is still putting up with it. That is no answer. If he has it at home, he has it elsewhere. It curses other people besides his family.

Mere enduring is no answer. I knew an imperious, rich woman, married to rather a gentle, almost saintly man. Her father told him when they were married that she was "a spirited girl, and you had better give her her head." They were married for more than fifty years. He put up with worldliness and materialism that might have been cured if early in their life he had taken with her the line he should have taken. Lots of times we "endure," not from any considered thought, but just because we don't want to make matters worse and we don't know what to do. Mere enduring is no answer.

Help to Cure

What if we decide we'd like to try at least to help cure the sin of another? Let me make a few suggestions:

First, let us always go to sinners as a sinner ourselves. Nobody in this world is in any position to condemn nor preach to others as if he stood somewhere above them. All of us in the Christian fellowship are sinners, forgiven sinners, but sinners first, last, and all the time.

It is Christ who is righteous, not we. It is he and his righteousness, not we or ours, that we try to hold up. A person honestly trying to follow him has something to say to one who is not, and he should say it, but with plenty of humility, knowing his own weakness. God can only use this, never our pretenses.

Second, let us pray for the person. We shall find that we cannot pray for him until we forgive him. If we try to pray when we feel proud and condemnatory, we simply will find ourselves unable to do it. It is impossible to pray to God about the sins of others till we have been honest about our own sins. This causes us to stand, not above the person for whom we pray, but beside him, where we belong—especially in the presence of God. Prayer may do very much to loosen up our own constricted and unyielding attitudes and may do the same for him.

Third, if it seems right, and when it seems right, let us go to him to try to talk things out. If there has been any wrong on our side, even in the way we have taken his wrongdoing, it may be well to begin with that; otherwise, we may seem to be coming in a spirit of condemnation.

We are not universally successful, but we are often successful, if we begin this way. It encourages the other person to be honest instead of defensive about his own wrongs. Our personal humility as against pride and self-righteousness, our humor and good nature when he expects a scolding, our awareness of our faults as well as his, all these will tend to get things opened up on the right basis.

Fourth, let us speak plainly about what has happened. If we are wrong about what we think are facts, let us be open to correction on them; yet we know, and he knows that wrong has been done. Let us not fear to put the right name to it, and to challenge him about it. It is terribly important that we keep the attitude of humility and the spirit of prayer all the way through. It is also important not to mince matters.

"The truth shall make you free." That means we must learn the truth, face the truth, and admit the truth—then it will make us free. Our tone of voice is important, as well as keeping self-justification out of it, and anything like recrimination. Bathed in prayer, and in a desire not to get even but to restore the relationship, frank speaking, "speaking the truth in love" as Paul calls it, can work wonders.

The Next Alternative

This course is not universally guaranteed to succeed, however, and there are times when an impartial, wise, and spiritually-minded third party may have to be called into the picture. Listen to these very concrete commands from our Lord himself:

> If your brother sins against you, go and tell him his fault, between you and him alone. If he listens to you, you have gained your brother. But if he does not listen, take one or two others along with you, that every word may be confirmed by the evidence of two or three witnesses. If he refuses to listen to them, tell it to the church

and if he refuses to listen even to the church, let him be to you as a Gentile and a tax-collector.

There is complete moral realism, and also a court of last resort. I would remind you that "telling it to the church" would not mean spreading it abroad by gossip but bringing it before a responsible company who would act like a jury in helping to find the truth and the justice of the situation.

If none of this works, we rest the case. We cast bitterness out of our hearts. We wait for the minor healing processes of time, and the major healing processes of prayer, to do their work. We bow to the imperfect human situation, and to the fact that we are not God with the whole answer in our hands.

But we do not consign the wrongdoer to limbo. We go on hoping and we go on praying. No Christian ever puts anybody else in a finally hopeless category. That, I think, is part of what Christ meant when he said, "Judge not." Do not put people in fixed and final categories, where you look upon them without hope.

There is the remaining matter of forgiveness. Our Lord spoke about few things so often. After he had given the Lord's Prayer, he went back to one petition of it, and said, "For if ye forgive not men their trespasses, neither will your heavenly Father forgive you your trespasses." That does not mean petulance on God's part, but God's recognition of his own law.

You and I will suffer for our withheld forgiveness. It will hurt us; it is bound to. Strictly speaking, we can only forgive one who recognizes that he has done us a wrong, and seeks to make it right, and asks us for forgiveness. But you and I can prevent this from happening by our censoriousness, general and gossipy criticism, our proud and self-righteous disdain toward him. It may be that before such a person can ask for forgiveness, he may need to feel in us forgivingness, readiness to forgive.

When a wrong has been done, it takes two to right it—the one who committed it and the one against whom it was committed. The spirit of hope for reconciliation, prayer that it may take place, the removal of all obstacles on our side—that is what constitutes "forgivingness." And a Christian must always strive to maintain it.

The truth is, no other human being is beyond redemption, and you and I in our own way may stand right now in just as much need of it as someone who has done clear and obvious wrong. Mindful of the indissoluble connection between God's forgiveness of us, and our forgiveness of one another, let us keep in mind what our Lord said:

Whenever you stand praying, forgive, if you have anything against anyone, so that your Father also who is in heaven may forgive you your trespasses.

And also what Paul said: "Let all bitterness and wrath and anger and clamor and slander be put away from you, and all malice, and be kind to one another, tender-hearted, forgiving one another, as God in Christ forgave you."

Contemporary Responses

17

Toward Ecclesial Practices and Notions of Authority That Embody Radical Hope

KIMBERLY PENNER[1]

Notions of communal authority and church discipline are central to Anabaptist-Mennonite theology and practice. Sixteenth-century Swiss and Dutch Anabaptists emphasized the disciplinary authority of the community of faith to strive for holiness and unity, most notably in the practice of the Lord's Supper. Influential early Anabaptist leader Balthasar Hubmaier rooted a basis for church discipline in the words of Jesus to his disciples, that whatever you bind or loose on earth will be bound or loosed in heaven (Matt 16:19; 18:18–20; John 20:21–23).[2] According to Hubmaier, and others after him, this meant that the church, with authority from Jesus, could forgive and condemn. This understanding of church discipline was eventually used to ban and excommunicate believers who would not repent and therefore could not be reconciled to the congregation.

The writers in this volume offer critical and constructive arguments in favor of a renewed emphasis on the authority of the community of faith and a repositioning of the authority of the pastor within that of the community. They also offer an understanding of church discipline as primarily restorative, rather than divisive and punitive. The questions they ask and respond to are important. How do Christians, specifically Anabaptist-Mennonites, understand authority as it pertains to the role of the pastor

---

1. Kimberly Penner is an adjunct instructor at Conrad Grebel University College and Victoria College, University of Toronto, Ontario.

2. See for example, Hubmaier, "On Fraternal Admonition," essay in this volume.

and of the congregation? Who grants it and what does it enable? What kind of discipline is the church called to practice?

In the decades since their work was initially published, new answers to these questions have emerged. Existing and historical notions of ecclesial authority and church discipline for Anabaptist-Mennonites have been re-evaluated with a critical eye for relationships of unequal power within the congregation in light of the experiences of Mennonites who have been marginalized, excluded, oppressed, and/or experienced violence within the church itself. Feminist theologians, for example, including Gloria Albrecht, Malinda Berry, Lydia Neufeld Harder, Carol Penner, and myself, have questioned and reimagined what is possible regarding the community of faith as a flat structure of shared authority, and the life-giving potential (or not) of Matt 18 for practices of church discipline.[3] Given its painful history as the cause of division and broken relationships, should discipline continue to be a practice in the life of the church? If so, how? By what criteria?

My response is informed by the commitments of liberationist theologies (including feminist, womanist, *mujerista*, liberation, black, queer, postcolonial, and disability), which necessarily attend to the experiences of the oppressed, marginalized, and disadvantaged and remain suspicious of all unequal relationships of power. I claim that notions of pastoral and communal authority for Anabaptist-Mennonites must name and subvert relationships of unequal, top down power, in order that each congregant's authority to minister, which may differ based on role and responsibilities, be embodied in ways that are liberating for all. In other words, existing church structures and policies are better able to engender a priesthood of all believers when the interpersonal and social systemic nature of privilege is understood as it pertains to the community of faith. I find that Keri Day's articulation of radical hope, as that which is both optimistic about our ability to embody relationships that model the kin-dom of God,[4] and also realistic about the existence and implications of unequal relationships of power among us, exemplifies

---

3. See for example, Albrecht, *Character of Our Communities*; Neufeld Harder, *Obedience, Suspicion*; Berry, "Shalom Political Theology"; C. Penner, "Content to Suffer"; and K. Penner, "Mennonite Peace Theology."

4. The phrase "kin-dom of God" is used by *mujerista* theologian Ada María Isasi-Díaz to liberate traditional understandings of the scriptural view of the Kingdom of God as a metaphor for a new world order from dominant and oppressive cultural experiences of society. Kin-dom refers to the liberation of God at work among people who are suffering and oppressed by kings. See Isasi-Díaz, "Kin-dom of God."

this commitment and thus serves as a guiding concept for conversations on church polity moving forward.

Priesthood of Believers

In section one of this volume, "On Pastoral Authority," writers name the ways in which they see the Mennonite Church losing its identity as a priesthood of all believers, or what one editorial comment refers to as the "ministerial patterns of the free-church tradition."[5] Writers argue, the Mennonite Church ought to return to an Anabaptist emphasis on the value of the congregation as a whole rather than a hierarchical, or "Protestant," model of church polity.[6] Gerald Studer suggests moving away from thinking of conferences as "the church" in favor of the local congregation as "church."[7] For many, the kind of renewal that the Mennonite Church (and Mennonite theology) needed following WWII was Anabaptist and sectarian. This return to a more Anabaptist view of church included a focus on the *essence* of church as a community of disciples modelling the ideal of the kingdom of God rather than the *structure* of church (especially not a hierarchical one).

While these concerns were, in some ways, highly contextual, the issue of pastoral and congregational authority and implications for church structure and polity remain. In 2017, delegates from across Canada voted to restructure Mennonite Church Canada in order to place increased responsibility on local congregations and the five regional churches (called area conferences in the United States): Mennonite Church Eastern Canada, Mennonite Church Manitoba, Mennonite Church Saskatchewan, Mennonite Church Alberta, and Mennonite Church British Columbia. This restructuring was motivated by several factors, including financial ones, but reflects an understanding of church as primarily local and not hierarchical. The conclusion of the Mennonite Church Canada discernment process on LGBTQ inclusion ("Being a Faithful Church") confirms an emphasis on the authority of the local congregation, compared to leaders at the conference level. According to "A Resolution to the Mennonite Church Canada Delegate Assembly July 2016: Being a Faithful Church," the "Being a Faithful Church" task force recommended that "we create space/leave room within

---

5. Unattributed "Marginalia" (excerpt, 1958), essay in this volume, 135.

6. See essays in this volume: Studer, "Second Thoughts;" unattributed "Marginalia" (excerpt 1958); Bakker, "Efficiency;" and Metzler, "Need."

7. Studer, "Second Thoughts," essay in this volume, 5.

our Body to test alternative understandings from that of the larger Body to see if they are a prophetic nudging of the Spirit of God."[8] Each congregation was given the freedom to discern for themselves the leading of the Holy Spirit with regard to the authority of the Confession of Faith in a Mennonite Perspective for same-sex relationships.[9]

I too see the value of the local congregation and of the authority of each person to discern the leading of the Holy Spirit for the community of faith. At the same time, I wonder, is it possible to escape hierarchical (unequal) church polity and structure on the local level, or anywhere? And if not, what are our criteria for figuring out whose experience is authoritative for ecclesial life and ethics in a given context? While some Anabaptist-Mennonites today might believe in an essentialist definition of church removed from the political and messy realities of institutional and social life, even if only as an ideal, a fellowship of believers wherever gathered is alway socially located within a matrix of intersecting relationships of power.[10] As a result, a certain realism that pays attention to relationships of power is required in order to live honestly and well together. I return to this issue later.

Pastoral Authority

What of the role and authority of the pastor as they pertain to this conversation? In section one of this volume, several writers identify a crisis in ministry, namely, the separation and valuing of clergy over and against laity. Walter Klaassen's contribution "New Presbyter Is Old Priest Writ Large" exemplifies this concern. According to Klaassen, the gap between clergy

8. Mennonite Church Canada, "Resolution."

9. The Introduction to the *Confession of Faith in a Mennonite Perspective* explains it "is the work of two Mennonite groups in North America, the Mennonite Church (MC) and the General Conference Mennonite Church (GC). [Since 2001 these two groups, with the Conference of Mennonites in Canada, have realigned to form Mennonite Church USA and Mennonite Church Canada.]" It is a guideline, not doctrine, for the interpretation of Scripture and for ethics.

10. My comment here is informed by an understanding of intersectionality—a theory that claims that systems of oppression (sexism, racism, heterosexism, classism, ableism) shape and influence one another in the lived experiences of diverse people (Kim and Shaw, *Intersectional Theology*, xvii). Intersectionality has its roots in the experiences of black women and black feminist thinkers such as Kimberlé Crenshaw, Patricia Hill Collins, Audre Lorde, Vivian May, Ange-Marie Hancock, Johanna Butler, bell hooks, and Beverly Guy-Sheftall.

and laity in Mennonite Churches resembles the relationship between the priest and the common people in the medieval church. A failure, he claims, of the Protestant Reformation to embody the theological shift that would give everyone equal access to God. Klaassen is particularly concerned with the implications for the pastor. The pastor, Klaassen writes, "must be above the normal aberrations of living; he may not have the passions we have; we expect him to be paternalistic, blessing us from his elevated sanctity; we expect him to be holy for us; we expect him to have all the answers to all the questions of life, and we expect him to give us clear, unequivocal, authoritative answers to these questions."[11] These expectations reflect an understanding of pastoral authority as the authority to discern and follow the leading of the Holy Spirit on behalf of, rather than together with, the rest of the congregation, and are therefore upsetting to Klaassen.

For Klaassen, this failure is both an Anabaptist and a Protestant one. From an Anabaptist perspective, Klaassen finds that it is highly problematic to expect the pastor to "be the church" for others. It conflicts with a discipleship ethic that, through baptism, requires every believer to commit to a life in and with Christ exemplified through both an inner and outer change. Therefore, an understanding of the significance of communal authority is important. From a Protestant perspective, the hierarchical view of clergy above laity he assumes is present fails to embody an emphasis on the priesthood of all believers that is "lying fallow" within Protestantism. For these reasons, the believers' authority to minister to one another within the congregation as shared and equally important, albeit with different roles and responsibilities, must be reclaimed.

I appreciate much of what Klaassen is arguing here. Yes, the church is called to be a priesthood of all believers and, therefore, a gap between clergy and laity is problematic. His depiction of the priesthood of all believers as congregants being priests to each other is particularly valuable. "The priesthood of all believers," he writes, "does not mean simply that we are our own priests in our access to God; it means that we, each one of us, are priests to each other. It means that God has put us in charge of each other so that . . . we will make ourselves responsible for the well-being of others around us."[12] Through faith, hope, and love we are called to live into these relationships of mutuality. But what of the power dynamics within the congregation that make relationships of mutuality challenging, if not dangerous?

11. Klaassen, "New Presbyter," essay in this volume, 46.
12. Klaassen, "New Presbyter," essay in this volume, 46.

Klaassen seems remarkably unaware of the various relationships of power operating within congregations and their implications for ministry. While Klaassen is critical of the unrealistic expectations being placed on pastors and, therefore, values a priesthood of all believers that shares roles and responsibilities, he nonetheless admires the men currently doing everything they can to meet the unrealistic expectations placed on them. He writes: "It is no wonder that young men refuse to be pushed into that kind of situation [the pastorate], but at the same time the men who do go into the ministry and work under that cruel handicap [of high expectations to be perfect] have my honest admiration."[13] He is concerned about burn out, but appears ignorant of the other potential risks of being placed on a pedestal.

When clergy are idolized as morally superior or holier than others, questions about intimacy, boundaries, power, sexual attraction, and unconscious motivations are overlooked and the potential for abuse to be perpetrated increases. An understanding of the pastor as morally superior also makes members of the congregation less likely to believe survivors of clergy abuse when they come forward. No one benefits from setting such unrealistic expectations of clergy, but the stakes are significantly higher than what Klaassen articulates.

A more accurate and accountable understanding of the role and authority of the pastor is one that not only reorients the pastor as one among many equally important people in the congregation for decision-making and leadership, but is realistic about what is possible and names the potential for the role to be misused (e.g., the potential to conflate spiritual intimacy and physical intimacy). I find Lydia Neufeld Harder's theology of ministry particularly helpful in this regard. She claims that while people ministering within the Mennonite faith tradition tend to identify most commonly with Jesus as a model for ministry, they should also identify with Jesus's disciples, who face temptations and need to be honest about and learn from failure. In the context of discipleship in the Gospel of Mark, she writes:

> Mark challenges us well to describe the present reality of ministry in the church honestly and without pretense, naming the differences in status and the need for recognition of the various ministering persons in the community. We are asked to describe the temptations and opportunities that are there within the present social and political realities for those who are officially named and

---

13. Klaassen, "New Presbyter," essay in this volume, 46.

for those who perform ministry more unofficially. We are challenged to be sensitive to God who frequently subverts the human evaluations and classifications of ministry, whether this means affirming our ministry when we feel it is unimportant or pointing us to the need for further teaching and healing.[14]

Harder's understanding of ministry, rooted in Scripture, is one that values mutuality and is also realistic about power. It acknowledges relationships of unequal power within the community of faith and between various ministers (official and unofficial). After acknowledging these differences, power can be shared in ways that empower those who are typically silenced to speak, encourage those who usually speak to listen, and, in doing so, work toward the betterment of all.

Church Discipline

The historical articles in this volume on church discipline and their interpretations of Matt 18 also benefit from a critical rereading with attention to relationships of power. I have mentioned how an uncritical view of the role of the clergy, as well as a view of the clergy as having power over others, can lead to abuse. Regarding church discipline and Matt 18, the issue is how processes of reconciliation can also perpetuate harm when relationships of power remain unexamined. Perpetrators of abuse are in positions of power that make it dangerous for victims to enter processes of reconciliation and healing through, especially, a one-on-one interaction with their abuser. While I appreciate the intention to use Matt 18 as a form of redemptive church discipline compared to traditional patterns of discipline resulting in excommunication/"the ban," and understand that for the time this was an important step, Matt 18-based articles like Elmer Ediger's review of "Studies in Church Discipline" do not go far enough in restoring both the victim and the offender. Likewise, while Balthasar Hubmaier, "On Fraternal Admonition" is realistic about the fallenness of humanity or "worldly sin," his vision of communal accountability and church discipline remains uncritical of the fallenness of the church itself.

When engaging these contributions on Matt 18 today, the dangers of focusing primarily on restoring the perpetrator to the community of faith with little awareness of the impacts of this process on survivors of abuse cannot be overstated. Survivor-centered policies are required for reporting

---

14. Neufeld Harder, "Mutuality of Ministry," 80.

and responding to abuse. Survivor-centered policies protect the survivor as they come forward by providing them with a way to submit allegations of abuse anonymously, to be able to avoid having their name shared with their alleged perpetrator if so desired, and with the assurance that a third party investigative agency that is also survivor-focused can be involved. Being survivor-centered means letting the survivor shape the narrative. Most often, it also includes public acknowledgment and apology by the institution involved and supporting the survivor if they choose to release their narrative to the public.[15] When survivor-centered policies for preventing and responding to abuse do not exist, notions of church discipline remain potential sources of trauma and harm.

Radical Hope

I have offered a critical view of unequal relationships of power within the church as they impact notions of pastoral and congregational authority and church discipline. I have consistently argued why it is important to be realistic about the contexts of privilege and disadvantage that have the potential to shape congregational life and why this does not mean that we should give up or lose hope. The concept that I find most helpful to better articulate this tension and to serve as a norm for congregational life moving forward is what womanist Keri Day refers to as "radical hope."

To radicalize hope is to "acknowledge that hope moves beyond feelings of mere optimism."[16] The precondition for hope is despair and brokenness. Therefore, hope includes an understanding of radical loss and what can and does go wrong within our experience and history. Even as it includes this awareness and realism about brokenness, "hope is the audacious conviction that genuine newness in history is possible. . . . These possible other futures are based on the radical social practices and defiant liberative projects of those who are marginalized, as these groups articulate new meanings of love, freedom, and justice."[17] They are optimistic and can imagine new realities,

---

15. I am grateful for Hilary Jerome Scarsella's work in survivor advocacy in the context of faith communities and consider her contributions to be valuable resources for the church. See for example "Bearing Witness."

16. Day, *Religious Resistance*, 162.

17. Day, *Religious Resistance*, 162.

but they are also realistic, based on an awareness of the current brokenness evident, for example, in existing systems of oppression.[18]

Lydia Neufeld Harder's theology of ministry embodies radical hope as it encourages ministers (official and unofficial) to consider the power dynamics that shape their lived experiences, to minister in ways that work toward shared power, and to be honest about the likelihood of failure. The disciples, as well as Jesus, are important models for ministry as they encourage ministers to confront their own humanity and the difference that social situatedness and relationships of power make for living into the role. I would add that it is also important to have models for ministry other than Jesus because of the important question, "Who has the privilege of being able to identify with Jesus?" Jesus's gender as well as depictions of his race and assumptions about his sexuality have made it difficult at best for many to see themselves reflected in Jesus.

Another person whose work promotes radical hope and offers practical examples of what it could look like is Malinda Berry. I highly recommend her three suggested practices for congregational life from her article, "Shalom Political Theology: A New Type of Mennonite Peace Theology." These three practices are: 1) naming influential members of faith communities as influential (rather than subscribing to a false sense of egalitarianism); 2) practicing nonviolent communication, "a communication process . . . that cultivates empathy and compassion as requisites for personal and communal well-being"; and 3) Circle Process—"a practice of creating a social container for all voices to be heard and valued."[19] Berry's theology addresses the fact that Anabaptist communities have not always been good at looking inward when it comes to practicing nonviolence. The theology she articulates in response, namely "shalom political theology," is a valuable resource for conversations about authority and discipline that seek to embody radical hope and nonviolence in ways that attend to sin and power.

Conclusion

The writers in this republication of *Concern* ask fundamental questions about the authority and role of the clergy and the congregation as well as discipleship and church discipline. They did so without liberationist perspectives, including, for example, the work of feminist Mennonite theologians. In light

---

18. Day, *Religious Resistance*, 162.
19. Berry, "Shalom Political Theology," 71.

of these perspectives, which demand attention to issues of systemic,[20] unequal, historical, contextual, and intersecting relationships of power within the church and society, it is important to name the inequalities in our relationships, to commit to dismantling them (considering the practical, political implications of our actions for those with the most at stake and guided by, for example, the virtues of solidarity and mutuality) and to embody radical hope for the church, including the liberation of all people from systems and relationships of domination and inequality.

---

20. By systemic, I mean "the patterned ways that violence is perpetuated and enabled with respect to broad collectives—institutions, religious groups, eras in history, dimensions of culture, and within the discourse itself" (Scarsella and Krehbiel, "Sexual Violence," 3). As Scarsella and Krehbiel point out, while the two are always intertwined, the interpersonal is often and problematically emphasized to the exclusion of the systemic. Both must be maintained.

18

The Ecclesial Flesh of Anabaptist Visions

ISAAC S. VILLEGAS[1]

A Missing Body

In the first volume of his *Mystic Fable*, Michel de Certeau characterizes the mystical discourses of the sixteenth and seventeenth centuries as emerging from grief, "an unaccepted mourning that has become the malady of bereavement, perhaps akin to the ailment melancholia."[2] After the ascension of Jesus, the material absence of his body birthed our faith as a kind of mystical desire. We are all like Mary Magdalene at the empty tomb: anguished and desperate to know Christ's whereabouts. "Since that time," de Certeau writes, "the believers have continued to wonder: 'Where art thou?' And from century to century they ask history as it passes: 'Where have you put him?' With events that are murmurings come from afar, with Christian discourses that codify the hermeneutics of new experiences, with community practices that render present a *caritas*, they 'invent' a mystic body—missing and sought after—that would be their own." This mystical desire pulses through our faith. "Christianity was founded upon *the loss of a body*—the loss of the body of Jesus Christ," de Certeau explains. "In the Christian tradition, an initial privation of body goes on producing

---

1. Isaac S. Villegas serves as a pastor at Chapel Hill Mennonite Fellowship in North Carolina and is the president of the NC Council of Churches. He writes as a columnist for *The Christian Century* and *Anabaptist World*.

2. De Certeau, *Mystic Fable*, 1.

institutions and discourses that are the effects of and substitutes for that absence: multiple ecclesiastical bodies, doctrinal bodies."[3]

The *Concern* articles in this book respond to that absence, the missing body—specifically the ecclesial body of Christ which, for these authors, has been in a process of slow disappearance since the sixteenth century. The assumption of these *Concern* writings is that after centuries of sacrilege, the Swiss Anabaptists rediscovered a faithful church. The Anabaptist movement reconstituted the body of Christ, absent since the early church, in time for the arrival of modernity. The radical reformers who emerged from Zwingli's circle in Zurich rendered present Christ's *caritas*, to use de Certeau's language, in communal commitments that served as a foundation for their reinstitution of the true evangelical faith.

Anabaptist Visions

The *Concern* movement's mid-twentieth-century turn to the sixteenth century followed a line of sight that Harold S. Bender opened up in his 1944 essay, "The Anabaptist Vision," where he defined authentic Anabaptism over against the other available Christian traditions: "For the Anabaptist, the church was neither an institution (Catholicism), nor the instrument of God for the proclamation of the divine Word (Lutheranism), nor a resource group for individual piety (Pietism). It was a brotherhood of love in which the fullness of the Christian life was expressed."[4] Bender counterposed his vision for a fellowship of noncoercive love against individualism and institutionalism. The next generation of Mennonites—this cohort who published reflections in the *Concern* pamphlets—took up the responsibility of outlining the practicalities of community life according to Bender's vision, while also criticizing the consolidation of administrative power in Mennonite institutions.[5] In his biography of Harold S. Bender, Albert Keim characterizes the relationship between the *Concern* movement and Bender as follows: "The young men were convinced that Bender and his generation had created a 'Corpus Mennoniticum' with little resemblance to the true Anabaptist vision."[6]

---

3. De Certeau, *Mystic Fable*, 81–82.
4. Bender, "Anabaptist Vision," 22.
5. Keim, "Bender and the *Concern* Group."
6. Keim, "Bender and the *Concern* Group," 454.

This selection of *Concern* articles develops the institutional change implied within the purview of Bender's vision. They flesh out the congregational and inter-congregational structures involved in Bender's "brotherhood of love," what de Certeau identified as practices of *caritas*. The authors attempted to make visible a vision, to delineate the practicalities for a community to re-present the body of Christ. Thus, as this collection demonstrates, discussions about church polity and discipline emerge as significant themes in the pamphlets. "No polity will ensure spirituality," Gerald C. Studer wrote, "but some polities are surely more conducive to true spirituality than others."[7]

The word has a form of life. The gospel happens in the flesh. Like the skeleton that structures the body, like the ligaments that connect the bones, and like the tissue that cradles organs, organizational concerns are essential topics for conversations about an Anabaptist vision. To debate the ramifications of the priestly function of each church member is the nature of a collective struggle to fashion a materialist vision for Anabaptism. These mid-twentieth-century arguments offer a glimpse into the thought-world of the generation after Bender as congregants negotiated appropriate material forms of ecclesial life—Mennonite congregational identity as a living and breathing version of the Anabaptist tradition. Everything was on the table for discussion, for debate, for revision: the role of ministers, the features of a worship service, the purpose of a denomination, the function of seminaries. These essays don't outline a program. Instead they center our attention on the need to discern institutional forms for the Anabaptist movement. They ask us to attend to the routines and rituals of a communal movement, the week-to-week organizational commitments of a vision for a way of life.

Structure matters. Formation matters. Practices matter. To ignore these themes allows contemporary authors to render the Anabaptist tradition into idealized values and essentialized distinctives—an Anabaptism articulated as quintessential characteristics abstracted from the practical matters of forming community life. Stuart Murray and Palmer Becker exemplify this tendency today. Both of them repeat, with some variation, Bender's vision.

Becker's pamphlet came first. Mennonite Mission Network published *What Is an Anabaptist Christian?* in 2008, in which Becker advocated for an identity based on "core values," as he named them. "The three principles

---

7. Studer, "Second Thoughts," essay in this volume, 7.

developed in this booklet are a modern-day adaptation of The Anabaptist Vision, a well-known statement made in 1943 by Harold S. Bender."[8] The purpose of his book was to define the essence of Anabaptism as a set of beliefs about behavior and belonging, without any account of Anabaptist forms of negotiating ecclesial life—no mention of everyday matters like mutual admonition, or who can serve and receive communion. In his 2010 book, *The Naked Anabaptist: The Bare Essentials of a Radical Faith*, Stuart Murray took the same approach: "What does Anabaptism look like when it is stripped down to the bare essentials?" he asked.[9] He considered the history of faith practices that form an ecclesial culture as religious husk that hide the Anabaptist kernel.[10]

Both Murray and Becker merely repeated Bender's approach to history, which Rodney James Sawatsky explained in *History & Ideology: American Mennonite Identity Definition through History* as an ideological tactic to develop a mythology of pristine Anabaptist origins, an essence to be used to bless or curse contemporary Mennonite identities. Sawatsky quoted Bender: "The great work which has been done by our scholars on the recovery of the Anabaptist vision and in the defining of the essence of Anabaptist theology," Bender wrote late in his career, "furnish[es] a critique of contemporary Mennonitism in the light of the best of the original tradition." Bender considered this original tradition, as constructed by modern historiography, to be an essence of Anabaptism that rises above "the changing tides of theology and ethics now operative" and stands in judgment against "the encrustations of our own later traditions, which are not a part of the original heritage."[11] Bender's project served to reify the faith of Mennonite communities into a commodified identity, an Anabaptist essence ready for comparison with

---

8. Becker, *What Is an Anabaptist*, 3. Becker rewrites this argument in his recent book, *Anabaptist Essentials*.

9. Murray, *Naked Anabaptist*, 48.

10. Murray's approach to Anabaptism mimics Adolf von Harnack's in his nineteenth-century classic, *What Is Christianity?*, a definitive text which cast the vision of liberal Protestantism. In the same way that Harnack attempted to discard the Jewishness of Jesus and the Catholicism of Christianity as husk (e.g., "Husk were the whole of the Jewish limitations attaching to Jesus's message," "Western Catholicism . . . a heap of rubbish," 180, 272), Murray tries to strip away the relevance of historical "accretions" of living Anabaptist communities (e.g., "to strip back the historical and cultural accretions from traditions that have persisted through the centuries," 43–44), as if in the contemporary styles of ecclesial life one does not glimpse a clarified vision, as if histories of faithfulness do not elucidate a tradition.

11. See Bender, "Role of Tradition," in Sawatsky, *History and Ideology*, 133–34.

other essentialized Christian traditions in the marketplace of religious ideas.[12] The unabashed sensationalism of the title and contents of Stuart Murray's book—*The Naked Anabaptist: Bare Essentials of a Radical Faith*—is Bender's project come of age as a commodity fetish.

An alternative hermeneutic would have been to consider living traditions as visions transfigured through history, an Anabaptist vision refracted and illuminated through lives of faithfulness—to approach ecclesial bodies as indispensable articulations of Anabaptist identities. Such a vantage point toward history would involve a posture of adoration toward living bodies, as if congregations offer revelations. Like medieval Catholicism developed mystical rituals of the adoration of Christ at the Communion table, the lives of historic Anabaptist communities would become sites of revelatory visions. I take Doris Janzen Longacre as pointing in this direction when she described a congregation's ordinary table fellowship as a site of holy devotion. "We say as much about how well we discern the Lord's body by the way we conduct potlucks, dinners, and banquets, as by how reverently we bow through the Eucharist," she wrote in the companion volume to her Mennonite Central Committee cookbook, *More With Less*.[13] Longacre considered the practicalities of sharing food, of cooking and hospitality—the home economics of congregational life—as revelatory of God's life made flesh. This reverence before the body assembled for commonplace rituals of church life is the requisite posture to discern the features of a people's identity. The materiality of such cultural practices is the spirituality of a Christian tradition. Material praxes are the deposits of faith—not as a distillation of an Anabaptism in the past reincarnated for the present, but an identity always renewed and remade among the people gathered in a community, re-forming their faith with all of their histories. A hybridized Anabaptist, a Mennonite mestizaje—faithful to the tradition through the

---

12. Stanley Hauerwas warns that Bender's approach commodifies Anabaptist faith, thus playing into the fetishization of Mennonite identity: "I am suggesting that something may already have gone wrong in Anabaptist life just to the extent that there is a need to discover what makes Anabaptists 'distinctive.' . . . 'Identity' becomes the commodification of one's history to give us something to sell in the religious market . . . by making a fetish of those aspects of your lives that seemed so important" (Hauerwas, "Whose Church?," 69–73).

13. Longacre, *Living More With Less*, 248. I'm grateful to Anna Weaver for tracking down this reference in her personal library during the COVID-19 pandemic when research libraries were unavailable to me. For more robust accounts of Longacre's contribution to Mennonite theology, see Berry, "'This Mark,'" and Guenther Loewen, "Personal Is Political."

union of polygenetic identities. Descriptions of Anabaptist visions should begin here, with a phenomenology of the holy jumble of congregational life. We start where we are: our churches awash in Mennonite theologies, our worship alive with Anabaptist visions.

To invite people to worship is how to share with others a Mennonite faith, an Anabaptist vision, with the promise that members of the body will not threaten visitors with violence because the Christian life centers on communion with Jesus, who taught his followers through word and deed not to kill people, even enemies. Weapons deny the hospitality of God. Violence contradicts the spiritual logic of worship. To bow reverently before another, whether member or stranger, friend or enemy, in adoration of God's presence, requires a rejection of violence and a commitment to greet the other with a gesture of peace—not only in church buildings, but in every part of life, for worship guides all of life into the reign of God.

This is not necessarily a Mennonite distinctive. Christians within other traditions have recognized nonviolence as central to life with God. There is no denominational trademark on the belief that Christian worship is an ethical posture of hospitality to the God who arrives with every image of the divine, each human being, as the Spirit reforms a community into Christ's flesh. What we have in this volume is a collection of arguments from and for the worship life of people who have experienced within Mennonite communities visions for setting up a form of life with Jesus, the one whose words and actions invited followers to honor God's presence in others, that every human being belongs to God, which is the theological truth constitutive of biblical nonviolence. The Anabaptism to which these authors turn our attention is an explication of the logic of a holistic style of a worshipful life in the wake of the life, death, resurrection, and ascension of Jesus.

Ecclesial Formation

To experience Anabaptist visions involves a people, an assembly. The church gathers to welcome the presence of Jesus through the power of the Holy Spirit for the world. The Christian body is, as Menno Simons wrote in 1544, "flesh of Christ's flesh and bone of his bone."[14] This belief entails a relational structural of mutual belonging where believers commit themselves to a life with Christ. Ecclesiology names the theological discourse about

---

14. Simons, "Brief Confession," 448.

the nature of the relationships that delineate the shape of the church. The *Concern* authors turned to this theme as the forgotten yet necessary context for discussions of Anabaptist visioning.

In his "Discipleship and Church Order," included in this volume, William Klassen explained that to sift through lived forms of faith in order to preserve reified essences was a decidedly un-Anabaptist methodology. "We have assumed that we can distinguish between the essence and the form of the church and (somewhat naively) assumed that we have the essence, irrespective of the form that it takes," Klassen observed. "Obviously, our ancestors rejected such a spiritualizing interpretation, and wrestled seriously with church order." Anabaptist faith is about form—materiality of practice, organizational structure, ecclesial culture. "In fact," Klassen continued, "one might even say that at the basis of the rift between the Reformation and Anabaptists lay the question of church order in the deeper theological sense."[15] Collective bodies communicate Anabaptist theologies. Thus church order was vital to these conversations among the *Concern* authors.

To ignore the structure of relationships that compose the church would be to leave existing dynamics intact. To ignore how power flows through a congregation is to leave undisturbed worldly patterns of authority. For the *Concern* authors, the Anabaptist movement had everything to do with a gospel that leveled hierarchies because the work of the Holy Spirit involves the ordination of all believers as priests. Baptism initiates a communal sharing in Christ's power. To live into the anticlerical egalitarianism of the Anabaptist vision requires negotiations about power dynamics that play out in the practical matters of church life. Those are the conversations that the *Concern* group would not let the Mennonite community at large overlook.

Their concerns develop from the Anabaptist emphasis on the priesthood of all believers. This theological praxis displays an ecclesiological vision in which community members declare with their lives the shared power of God's grace. As Walter Klassen explained in an article in this volume, "The priesthood of all believers does not mean simply that we are our own priests in our access to God; it means that we, each one of us, are priests to each other," for "Christ is incarnated in us today in our relations with others."[16] The relational connections within the body of Christ mediate God's presence. Our status as priests does not justify the privatization of

---

15. Klassen, "Discipleship," essay in this volume, 41.
16. Klassen, "New Presbyter," essay in this volume, 47.

faith, as if people experience God independently from one another. Instead, each person offers grace for others.

Furthermore, this priestly function of every member entails a shared commitment for the well-being of the community, since priests are ordained to tend to the wholeness of the people before God. Thus the responsibility for mutual accountability, as William Klassen interpreted the believer's participation in Christ's priesthood: "for the church truly to be the church it must have authority to forgive and retain sins—an authority given to it as a body by Christ Himself (John 20:20, Matt 18:15)."[17] He cited two passages central to the Anabaptist tradition of church discipline, of binding and loosing, where God authorizes members of the body to address sin within the community. Matthew 18 and John 20 have guided the protocols of mutual admonition since the beginnings of Anabaptism. "Every disciple of Christ has a word from God," Klassen explained their theological significance. "This word is both conviction and forgiveness." While the hope for such a disciplinary process is restoration, Klassen noted the function of excommunication for the collective health of the body of Christ. He turned to the apostle Paul's counsel in 1 Cor 5:

> The incestuous man is to be removed from [the Corinthian church], but this is an action which requires the assembly.... The goal is the ultimate salvation of the transgressor, but in the meantime no words are spared to make it clear to the individual that he is officially transferred from Christ's kingdom to the domain of Satan.... The desire for the faithful church must always go hand in hand with being a witnessing community. The church is a witnessing community and anything which mars its testimony must be taken with utmost seriousness.

Church discipline may lead to forgiveness and reconciliation, or the process may result in the expulsion of an unrepentant person who has violated the community. "Drive out the wicked person from among you," the apostle Paul concluded his guidance (1 Cor 5:13).[18]

For Balthasar Hubmaier, in his "On Fraternal Admonition," church discipline is a discernment process that hopes for restoration of the sinner yet includes the possibility of the ban. Mutual admonition is an ecclesial practice

---

17. Klassen, "Some Neglected Aspects," essay in this volume, 92.

18. Paul does not invent this counsel; rather, he seems to be offering an interpretation of a consistent theme from God's law in Deuteronomy: see Deut 13:5; 17:7; 19:19; 21:21; 22:21, 24; 24:7.

of "wholesome medicine," Hubmaier wrote, that at times requires the amputation of an infected limb in order to save the life of the body. With the inclusion of this sixteenth-century treatise, the *Concern* editors returned to a vision for the integrated health of the church body. "Yes, even water baptism and the breaking of bread are vain, pointless and fruitless," Hubmaier explained, "if fraternal admonition and the Christian ban do not accompany them, admonition belonging to baptism as the ban belongs to communion and fellowship." Admonition and excommunication provide the framework for the interconnected practices that define an Anabaptist ecclesiology, the communal structure that makes visible the body of Christ.[19]

This volume on church life returns us to a concern for "community practices that render present a *caritas*," to borrow again de Certeau's words. These writings turn our attention to an era when Christians sought "a mystic body—missing and sought after—that would be their own."[20] I take these mid-twentieth-century reflections as an expression of this mystical longing for Christ's ascended body. The authors grasp at a vision of Jesus, God's incarnate presence, by means of the habits that structure a communal life—to be transfigured, as a collective body, through the Spirit; that earthly life would become divine life, God's will on earth as it is in heaven. These pages sketch the routines of ordinary mysticism, of discerning the form of the body, the material life of the community, in order to join the self to others in communion with Christ. Their words are prayers, supplications for all of us to find ourselves held in God's grace made flesh.[21]

---

19. Hubmaier, "On Fraternal Admonition," essay in this volume, 109. It was a failure of John H. Yoder's formulation of "binding and loosing" for the *Concern* group—which he repeated throughout his career—to ignore the Anabaptist integration of Jesus's teaching about mutual admonition in Matt 18 with Paul's counsel regarding excommunication in 1 Cor 5. Yoder's vision for church discipline prioritized the reconciliation of the sinner without concern for the person sinned against. See my "Ecclesial Ethics," especially the section entitled, "Protocols Redacted."

20. De Certeau, *Mystic Fable*, 81–82.

21. Williams, *Why Study the Past?*, 96: "the Christian seeking to understand the Christian past as a believer not only as an historian has very specially the task of trying to stand with Christians in an earlier age in their prayer."

APPENDIX

Concern Republication Volumes

The original Concern pamphlet series consisted of eighteen volumes that were published between 1954 and 1971. What follows in this index is a complete listing of that content as reorganized in the seven-volume series published by Wipf and Stock.

The Roots of Concern: Writings on Anabaptist Renewal 1952–1957, ed. Virgil Vogt. Eugene, OR: Wipf & Stock, 2009.

Concern for Education: Essays on Christian Higher Education, 1958–1966, ed. Virgil Vogt. Eugene, OR: Wipf & Stock, 2010.

Concern for the Church in the World: Essays on Christian Responsibility, 1958–1963, ed. Laura Schmidt Roberts. Eugene, OR: Wipf & Stock, 2022.

Concern for Church Renewal: Essays on Community and Discipleship, 1958–1966, ed. Laura Schmidt Roberts. Eugene, OR: Wipf & Stock, 2022.

Concern for Church Mission and Spiritual Gifts: Essays on Faith and Culture, 1958–1968, ed. Laura Schmidt Roberts. Eugene, OR: Wipf & Stock, 2022.

Concern for Church Polity and Discipline: Essays on Pastoral Ministry and Communal Authority, 1958–1969, ed. Laura Schmidt Roberts. Eugene, OR: Wipf & Stock, 2022.

APPENDIX: *CONCERN* REPUBLICATION VOLUMES

Concern *for Anabaptist Renewal: A Radical Reformation Reader, 1971*, ed. Virgil Vogt and Laura Schmidt Roberts. Eugene, OR: Wipf & Stock, 2022.

***The Roots of* Concern: *Writings on Anabaptist Renewal 1952–1957*,** ed. Virgil Vogt. Eugene, OR: Wipf & Stock, 2009.

   Virgil Vogt, "Foreword"

   Paul Peachey, "The Historical Genesis of the Concern Project"

   The Original Frontispiece of Concern Volumes 1–4

Concern 1 (1954)

   Paul Peachey, "Introduction"

   Paul Peachey, "Toward an Understanding of the Decline of the West"

   John Howard Yoder, "The Anabaptist Dissent: The Logic of the Place of the Disciple in Society"

Concern 2 (1955)

   Paul Peachey, "Preface"

   John W. Miller, "The Church in the Old Testament"

   Paul Peachey, "Spirit and Form in the Church of Christ"

   David A. Shank and John Howard Yoder, "Biblicism and the Church"

   Appendix: "Close communion—On what lines?"

Concern 3 (1956)

   Paul Peachey, "Preface"

   C. Norman Kraus and John W. Miller, "Intimations of Another Way: A Progress Report"

   Hans-Joachim Wiehler, "Preaching in the Church?"

   J. Lester Brubaker and Sol Yoder, "A Concern Retreat [Concern and Camp Luz]"

   Lewis Benson, "The Call: Journal of Spiritual Reformation"

   Notes on books

APPENDIX: *CONCERN* REPUBLICATION VOLUMES

Concern 4 (June 1957)

Paul Peachey, "Preface"

"Epistolary: An Exchange by Letter"

Paul Peachey, "What Is Concern?"

John Howard Yoder, "What Are Our Concerns?"

John W. Miller, "Organization and Church"

Herbert Klassen, "Property: A Problem in Christian Ethics"

Concern *for Education: Essays on Christian Higher Education, 1958–1966*, ed. Virgil Vogt. Eugene, OR: Wipf & Stock, 2010.

Virgil Vogt, "Editor's Note"

Michael Cartwright, "Foreword"

John Howard Yoder, "Christian Education: Doctrinal Orientation" (1959)

John Howard Yoder, "A Syllabus of Issues Facing the Church College" (1964)

John Howard Yoder and Paul M. Lederach, "Theological Statements for a Philosophy of Mennonite Education" (1971)

Concern 13 (1966)

Albert J. Meyer and Walter Klaassen, "Church and Mennonite Colleges"

Joanne Zerger Janzen, "The Bethel Experience in Retrospect"

Walter Klaassen, "Christian Life at Conrad Grebel College"

Henry Rempel, "The Bluffton College Christian Fellowship"

Steve Behrends, "Christian Communal Living on the Tabor Campus"

[Unattributed] "Tabor Christian Fellowship Association"

Glenn M. Lehman, "The Church on Eastern Mennonite College Campus"

Harold E. Bauman, "The Church on Campus, Present and Future: What are the Issues?"

Virgil Vogt, "Afterword"

APPENDIX: *CONCERN* REPUBLICATION VOLUMES

Concern *for the Church in the World: Essays on Christian Responsibility, 1958–1963*, ed. Laura Schmidt Roberts. Eugene, OR: Wipf & Stock, 2022.

Laura Schmidt Roberts, "Series Foreword"

Laura Schmidt Roberts, "Introduction"

Gordon D. Kaufman, "Nonresistance and Responsibility" (Concern 6, 1958)

Albert J. Meyer, "A Second Look at Responsibility" (Concern 6)

David Habegger, "Nonresistance and Responsibility—A Critical Analysis" (Concern 7, 1959)

John Howard Yoder, "The Otherness of the Church" (Concern 8, 1960)

Concern 10 (1961)

Jan M. Lochmann, "Christian Thought in the Age of the Cold War"

Albert Gaillard, "Christians and Marxists"

Katharina van Drimmelen, "Where Are the Firemen?"

John Howard Yoder, "The Christian Answer to Communism"

John Howard Yoder, "Marginalia"

Concern 11 (1963)

Karl Barth, "Poverty"

Andrew Murray, "The Poverty of Christ"

R. Mehl, "Money"

Virgil Vogt, "God or Mammon"

John Howard Yoder, "Marginalia"

Melissa Florer-Bixler, "All Economy Is Atheist: Towards a Non-Competitive Hope for the Church in the World"

Appendix: Concern republication volumes content list

APPENDIX: *CONCERN* REPUBLICATION VOLUMES

CONCERN *for Church Renewal: Essays on Community and Discipleship, 1958–1966*, ed. Laura Schmidt Roberts. Eugene, OR: Wipf & Stock, 2022.

Laura Schmidt Roberts, "Series Foreword"

Laura Schmidt Roberts, "Introduction"

John Howard Yoder, "Marginalia" excerpt (CONCERN 8, 1960)

John Howard Yoder, "Marginalia" excerpt (CONCERN 5, 1958)

Hans-Ruedi Weber, "The Church in the House" (CONCERN 5)

Quintus Leatherman, "The House Church in the New Testament" (CONCERN 5)

Paul M. Miller, "Can the Sunday School Class Be the 'House' within which the True Church Is Experienced?" (CONCERN 5)

Albert Steiner, "Group Dynamics in Evangelism [by Paul Miller]: A Review Article" (CONCERN 8)

Gerald C. Studer, "Evangelism Through the Dynamics of a Christian Group" (CONCERN 5)

Virgil Vogt, "Small Congregations" (CONCERN 5)

CONCERN 12 (1966)

Leland Harder, "Changing Forms of the Church and Her Witness"

John W. Miller, "The Renewal of the Church"

John Howard Yoder, "Marginalia: A Syllabus of Issues"

Lewis Benson, "The Order that Belongs to the Gospel" (CONCERN 7, 1959)

Susanne Guenther Loewen, "After Yoder: Failure, Authenticity, and the Renewal of the Mennonite Church"

César García, "A Global Communion as a Condition for the Possibility of Church Renewal"

Appendix: CONCERN republication volumes content list

APPENDIX: *CONCERN REPUBLICATION VOLUMES*

CONCERN *for Church Mission and Spiritual Gifts: Essays on Faith and Culture, 1958–1968*, ed. Laura Schmidt Roberts. Eugene, OR: Wipf & Stock, 2022.

    Laura Schmidt Roberts, "Series Foreword"

    Laura Schmidt Roberts, "Introduction"

    Paul Peachey, "Churchless Christianity" (CONCERN 7, 1959)

    M. H. Grumm, "The Search for Guaranteed Survival" (CONCERN 8, 1960)

    Edmund Perry, "The Christian Mission to the Resurgent Religions" (CONCERN 9, 1961)

    John Howard Yoder, "A Light to the Nations" (CONCERN 9)

    Paul Peachey, "The End of Christendom" (CONCERN 9)

CONCERN 15 (1967)

    John Howard Yoder, "Marginalia"

    James Fairfield, "Tongues, a Testimony"

    Herb Klassen and Maureen Klassen "You Shall Receive . . . "

    S. Djojodihardijo, "An Experience in My Life"

    Donald R. Jacobs, "The Charismatic in East Africa"

    Myron S. Augsburger, "The Charismatic Aspects of the Work of the Spirit"

    Irvin B. Horst, "A Historical Estimate of the Charismatic Movement"

    Gerald C. Studer, "The Charismatic Revival: A Survey of the Literature"

    Werner Schmauch, "The Prophetic Office in the Church" (CONCERN 5, 1958)

CONCERN 16 (1968)

    Henderson Nylrod, "Nasty Noel"

    William Roberts Miller, "Pious Jingle Bells and the Coming of Christ"

    Marlin Jeschke, "Getting Christ Back Out of Christmas"

    John Howard Yoder, "On the Meaning of Christmas"

John Howard Yoder and Virgil Vogt, "Marginalia:
The Case Against Christmas"

Hyung Jin Kim Sun, "Global Anabaptist Movement:
From Cross-cultural to Multicultural to Intercultural"

Andrés Pacheco Lozano, "Mission and Margin(alization): An Ecumenically-Shaped Anabaptist/Mennonite Approach to Mission"

Appendix: CONCERN republication volumes content list

CONCERN *for Church Polity and Discipline: Essays on Pastoral Ministry and Communal Authority, 1958–1969*, ed. Laura Schmidt Roberts. Eugene, OR: Wipf & Stock, 2022.

Laura Schmidt Roberts, "Series Foreword"

Laura Schmidt Roberts, "Introduction"

Gerald C. Studer, "Second Thoughts on the Pastoral Ministry" (CONCERN 6, 1958)

[Unattributed] "Marginalia" excerpt (CONCERN 6)

A. H. A. Bakker, "Efficiency in the Church" (CONCERN 7, 1959)

Edgar Metzler, "The Need to Which We Minister" (CONCERN 7)

Lewis Benson, "The Church's One Foundation" (CONCERN 8, 1960)

Walter Klaassen, "The Preacher and Preaching" (CONCERN 9, 1961)

William Klassen, "Discipleship and Church Order: A Review and Discussion" (CONCERN 9)

Walter Klaassen, "New Presbyter Is Old Priest Write Large" (CONCERN 17, 1969)

J. Lawrence Burkholder, "Theological Education for the Believers' Church" (CONCERN 17)

Virgil Vogt, "Marginalia" excerpt (CONCERN 17)

Elmer Ediger, "*Studies in Church Discipline*: A Review Article" (CONCERN 5, 1958)

William Klassen, "Some Neglected Aspects in the Biblical View of the Church" (CONCERN 8)

APPENDIX: *CONCERN REPUBLICATION VOLUMES*

Calvin Redekop, "Postulates Concerning Religious Intentional Ethnic Groups" (CONCERN 9)

Balthasar Hubmaier, "On Fraternal Admonition" (CONCERN 14, 1967)

Don Jacobs, "Walking Together in East Africa" (CONCERN 14)

Samuel Shoemaker, "Dealing with Other People's Sins" (CONCERN 14)

Kimberly Penner, "Toward Ecclesial Practices and Notions of Authority that Embody Radical Hope"

Isaac S. Villegas, "The Ecclesial Flesh of Anabaptist Visions"

Appendix: CONCERN republication volumes content list

CONCERN *for Anabaptist Renewal: A Radical Reformation Reader, 1971*, ed. Virgil Vogt and Laura Schmidt Roberts. Eugene, OR: Wipf & Stock, 2022.

Editor's Note

John Roth, "Foreword"

CONCERN 18 (1971)

Virgil Vogt, "Introduction"

John Howard Yoder, "The Recovery of the Anabaptist Vision"

Harold S. Bender, "The Mennonite Conception of the Church and Its Relation to Community Building"

Harold S. Bender, "The Anabaptist Theology of Discipleship"

William Klassen, "Anabaptist Studies"

Walter Klaassen, "Radical Reformation"

Harold S. Bender, "The Pacifism of the Sixteenth Century Anabaptists"

"Anabaptism: An Introductory Bibliography"

Appendix: CONCERN republication volumes content list

Bibliography

Albrecht, Gloria. *The Character of Our Communities: Toward an Ethic of Liberation for the Church*. Nashville: Abingdon, 1995.

Anabaptist Mennonite Biblical Seminary. "AMBS Response to Victims of John H. Yoder Abuse." https://www.ambs.edu/about/ambs-response-to-victims-of-yoder-abuse.

Becker, Palmer. *Anabaptist Essentials: Ten Signs of a Unique Christian Faith*. Harrisonburg, VA: Herald, 2017.

———. *What Is an Anabaptist Christian?* Elkhart: Mennonite Mission Network, 2010.

Bender, Harold S. "The Anabaptist Vision." *Church History* 13.1 (March 1944) 3–24.

———. "Ministry." In *The Mennonite Encyclopedia*, edited by Harold S. Bender et al., 3:699–704. Scottdale: Mennonite Publishing House, 1957.

Berry, Malinda Elizabeth. "Shalom Political Theology: A New Type of Mennonite Peace Theology for a New Era of Discipleship." *The Conrad Grebel Review* 34.1 (2016) 49–75.

———. "'This Mark of a Standing Human Figure Poised to Embrace': A Constructive Theology of Social Responsibility, Nonviolence, and Nonconformity." PhD diss., Union Theological Seminary, 2013.

Bohren, Rudolf. *Das Problem der Kirchenzucht im Neuen Testament*. Zurich: Zollikon, 1952.

Confession of Faith in a Mennonite Perspective. Waterloo: Herald, 1995.

Cramer, David, et al. "Theology and Misconduct: The Case of John Howard Yoder." *The Christian Century* 131.17 (2014). https://www.christiancentury.org/article/2014-07/theology-and-misconduct.

Cranfield, C. E. B. "Divine and Human Action: The Biblical Concept of Worship." *Interpretation* 12.4 (1958) 387–98.

Davis, Leroy A. "The Parochial Syndrome." *The Christian Century* 82.50 (1965) 1543–45.

Day, Keri. *Religious Resistance to Neoliberalism: Womanist and Black Feminist Perspectives*. London: Palgrave Macmillan, 2016.

De Certeau, Michel. *The Mystic Fable, Vol. 1: The Sixteenth and Seventeenth Centuries*. Translated by Michael B. Smith. Chicago: The University of Chicago Press, 1992.

De Dietrich, Suzanne. *The Witnessing Community: The Biblical Record of God's Purpose*. Philadelphia: Westminster, 1958.

Dillistone, Frederick W. "Editorial." *Theology Today* 16.1 (1959) 4–7.

BIBLIOGRAPHY

Dyck, Cornelius J. "Early Ideas of Authority." In *Studies in Church Discipline*, edited by Maynard Shelly, 35–56. Newton: General Conference Mennonite Church, 1955.

———. "Love Working Through People." In *Studies in Church Discipline*, edited by Maynard Shelly, 7–12. Newton: General Conference Mennonite Church, 1955.

Dyck, Peter J. "The General Conference Approach to the Believers' Church." In *The Church, the Gospel, and War: A Report of the General Conference Peace Study Conference*, General Conference Mennonite Church, D70–D77. Newton: Board of Christian Service, General Conference Mennonite Church, 1953.

Eichholz, Georg. *Was heisst charismatische Gemeinde?: 1 Korinther 12*. Munchen: Kaiser, 1960.

Ewert, Marvin. "Personality and Discipline." In *Studies in Church Discipline*, edited by Maynard Shelly, 97–104. Newton: General Conference Mennonite Church, 1955.

Fox, George. *The Journals of George Fox*. 8th ed. 2 vols. London: London Friends' Tract Association, 1891.

———. *The Works of George Fox*. 8 vols. Philadelphia: Gould, 1831.

Friesen, Jacob T. "Where Do We Begin?" In *Studies in Church Discipline*, edited by Maynard Shelly, 115–30. Newton: General Conference Mennonite Church, 1955.

Friesen, Jacob T., and Maynard Shelly. "Introduction." In *Studies in Church Discipline*, edited by Maynard Shelly, ix–xii. Newton: General Conference Mennonite Church, 1955.

General Conference Mennonite Church (GCMC). *Proceedings of the Study Conference on the Believers' Church Held at Mennonite Biblical Seminary, Chicago, Illinois, August 23-25, 1955*. Newton: General Conference Mennonite Church, 1955.

———. "Toward a Revived Peace Position in Our Conference." In *The Church, the Gospel, and War: A Report of the General Conference Peace Study Conference*, E16–E20. Newton: Board of Christian Service, General Conference Mennonite Church, 1953.

Guenther Loewen, Susanne. "The Personal Is Political: The Politics of Liberation in Mennonite-Feminist Theologies." *Political Theology* 22.3 (2021) 192–210.

Hauerwas, Stanley. "Whose Church? Which Future? Whither the Anabaptist Vision?" In *In Good Company: The Church as Polis*, 65–78. Notre Dame: University of Notre Dame, 1995.

Hershberger, Nathan. "Power, Tradition, and Renewal: The *Concern* Movement and the Fragmented Institutionalization of Mennonite Life." *Mennonite Quarterly Review* 87.2 (2013) 155–86.

Hubmaier, Balthasar. "On Fraternal Admonition." In *Balthesar Hubmaier: Theologian of Anabaptism*. Translated and edited by H. Wayne Pipkin and John H. Yoder, 372–85. Scottdale: Herald, 1989.

Isasi-Díaz, Ada María. "Kin-dom of God: A Mujerista Proposal." In *In Our Own Voices: Latina/o Renditions of Theology*, edited by Benjamín Valentín, 171–90. Maryknoll: Orbis, 2010.

Jacob, George Andrew. *The Ecclesiastical Polity of the New Testament: A Study for the Present Crisis in the Church of England*. New York: T. Whittaker, 1872.

Keim, Albert N. "Bender and the *Concern* Group." In *Harold S. Bender, 1897-1962*, 450–71. Scottdale: Herald, 1998.

Kim, Grace Ji-Sun, and Susan M. Shaw. *Intersectional Theology: An Introductory Guide*. Minneapolis: Fortress, 2018.

Kraemer, Hendrik. *A Theology of the Laity*. Philadelphia: Westminster, 1958.

Krahn, Cornelius. "Menno and Discipleship." In *Studies in Church Discipline*, edited by Maynard Shelly, 63–80. Newton: General Conference Mennonite Church, 1955.

Kreider, A. E. "Standards with Love." In *Studies in Church Discipline*, edited by Maynard Shelly, 105–12. Newton: General Conference Mennonite Church, 1955.

Kreider, Robert. "Brotherly Discipline by the Early Swiss." In *Studies in Church Discipline*, edited by Maynard Shelly, 57–62. Newton: General Conference Mennonite Church, 1955.

Littell, Frank H. *The Anabaptist View of the Church*. Boston: Beacon, 1957.

Longacre, Doris Janzen. *Living More With Less*. Scottdale: Herald, 1980.

"Marginalia." *Concern* 6 (1958) 46–49.

Mennonite Church Canada. "A Resolution to the Mennonite Church Canada Delegate Assembly July 2016: Being a Faithful Church." https://www.commonword.ca/ResourceView/82/19085.

Meyer, Rudolph. "περιτέμνω, περιτομή, ἀπερίτμητος." In *Theologisches Worterbuch zum Neuen Testament: Pe-R*, edited by Gerhard Kittel, 6:72–84. Germany: Kohlhammer, 1959.

Milton, John. *Complete Poems and Major Prose*. New York: Odyssey, 1957.

Murray, Stuart. *The Naked Anabaptist: The Bare Essentials of a Radical Faith*. Scottdale: Herald, 2010.

Neufeld Harder, Lydia. "The Mutuality of Ministry: A Dialogue with Mark." In *Understanding Ministerial Leadership: Essays Contributing to a Developing Theology of Ministry*, edited by John A. Esau, 70–81. Eugene, OR: Wipf & Stock, 2017.

———. *Obedience, Suspicion, and the Gospel of Mark: A Mennonite Feminist Exploration of Biblical Authority*. Waterloo: Wilfred Laurier University Press, 1998.

Niebuhr, H. Richard. *The Purpose of the Church and Its Ministry: Reflections on the Aims of Theological Education*. New York: Harper, 1956.

Nisbet, Robert A. *The Quest for Community: A Study in the Ethics of Order and Freedom*. New York: Oxford University Press, 1953.

Penner, Carol. "Content to Suffer: An Exploration of Mennonite Theology from the Context of Violence Against Women." In *Peace Theology and Violence against Women*, edited by Elizabeth G. Yoder, 99–111. Elkhart: Institute of Mennonite Studies, 1992.

Penner, Kimberly. "Mennonite Peace Theology and Violence Against Women." *The Conrad Grebel Review* 35.3 (2017) 280–91.

Poettcker, Henry. "The New Testament Community." In *Studies in Church Discipline*, edited by Maynard Shelly, 13–34. Newton: General Conference Mennonite Church, 1955.

Price, Tom. "A Known Secret: Church Slow to Explore Rumors Against Leader." *The Elkhart Truth*, July 14, 1992. https://peacetheology.net/john-h-yoder/john-howard-yoder's-sexual-misconduct—part-three/.

———. "Teachings Tested: Forgiveness, Reconciliation in Discipline." *The Elkhart Truth*, July 16, 1992. https://peacetheology.net/john-h-yoder/john-howard-yoder's-sexual-misconduct—part-five/.

———. "Theologian Accused: Women Report Instances of Inappropriate Conduct." *The Elkhart Truth*. July 13, 1992. https://peacetheology.net/john-h-yoder/john-howard-yoder's-sexual-misconduct—part-two/.

———. "Theologian Cited in Sex Inquiry." *The Elkhart Truth*, June 29, 1992. https://peacetheology.net/john-h-yoder/john-howard-yoder's-sexual-misconduct—introductory-article/.

———. "Theologian's Future Faces a 'Litmus Test': Yoder's response to Allegations Counld Determine Standing in Field." *The Elkhart Truth*, July 12, 1992. https://peacetheology.net/john-h-yoder/john-howard-yoder's-sexual-misconduct—part-one/.

———. "Yoder's Actions Framed in Writings." *The Elkhart Truth*, July 15, 1992. https://peacetheology.net/john-h-yoder/john-howard-yoder's-sexual-misconduct—part-four/.

Sawatsky, Rodney. "Editorial." *The Conrad Grebel Review* 8.2 (1990) iii–iv.

———. *History and Ideology: American Mennonite Identity Definition through History*. Kitchener: Pandora, 2005.

Scarsella, Hilary Jerome. "Bearing Witness to Jesus, Resurrected Survivor of Sexual Violence." In *Liberating the Politics of Jesus: Renewing Peace Theology Through the Wisdom of Women*, edited by Elizabeth Soto Albrecht and Darryl W. Stephens, 151–66. London: Bloomsbury, 2020.

Scarsella, Hilary Jerome, and Stephanie Krehbiel. "Sexual Violence: Christian Theological Legacies and Responsibilities." *Religion Compass* 13 (2019). https://doi.org/10.1111/rec3.12337.

Schweizer, Eduard. *Gemeinde und Gemeindeordnung im Neuen Testament*. Zurich: Zwingli Verlag, 1959.

———. *Lordship and Discipleship*. Studies in Biblical Theology 28. London: SCM, 1960.

Shoemaker, Sam. *Extraordinary Living for Ordinary Men*. Grand Rapids: Zondervan, 1965.

Simons, Menno. "Brief Confession on the Incarnation." In *The Complete Writings of Menno Simons*, translated by Leonard Verduin, 422–54. Scottdale: Herald, 1956.

Smucker, J. N. "The Disciplined Life." In *Studies in Church Discipline*, edited by Maynard Shelly, 3–6. Newton: General Conference Mennonite Church, 1955.

Soto Albrecht, Elizabeth, and Darryl W. Stephens, eds. *Liberating the Politics of Jesus: Renewing Peace Theology through the Wisdom of Women*. London: T. & T. Clark, 2020.

Sullivan, Harry Stack. *The Interpersonal Theory of Psychiatry*. New York: Norton, 1953.

Toews, Paul. *Mennonites in American Society, 1930–1970: Modernity and the Persistence of Religious Community*. Scottdale: Herald, 1996.

Villegas, Isaac Samuel. "The Ecclesial Ethics of John H. Yoder's Abuse." *Modern Theology* 37.1 (2021) 191–214.

Vogt, Virgil, and Laura Schmidt Roberts, eds. *Concern for Anabaptist Renewal: A Radical Reformation Reader, 1971*. Eugene, OR: Wipf & Stock, 2022.

Vogt, Virgil, ed. *CONCERN for Education: Essays on Christian Higher Education, 1958–1966*. Eugene, OR: Wipf & Stock, 2010.

———. *The Roots of CONCERN: Writings on Anabaptist Renewal, 1952–1957*. Eugene, OR: Wipf & Stock, 2009.

Von Harnack, Adolf. *What Is Christianity?* 1957. Reprint, Philadelphia: Fortress, 1986.

Waltner Goossen, Rachel. "'Defanging the Beast': Mennonite Responses to John Howard Yoder's Sexual Abuse." *Mennonite Quarterly Review* 89.1 (2015) 7–80.

Williams, Rowan. *Why Study the Past? The Quest for the Historical Church*. Grand Rapids: Eerdmans, 2005.

Wise, Carroll A. *Pastoral Counseling: Its Theory and Practice*. New York: Harper, 1951.

Yoder, John Howard. *The Fullness of Christ: Paul's Vision of Universal Ministry*. 1987. Eugene, OR: Wipf & Stock, 2019.

www.ingramcontent.com/pod-product-compliance
Lightning Source LLC
Chambersburg PA
CBHW070918180426
43192CB00038B/1744